## Praise for #1 Bestselling Author Joe Bovino's First Book, *Field Guide to Chicks of the United States*

### Judge, 2013 Global eBook Awards (Gold Medal, Humor)

The illustrations were fantastic. The book was hilarious. I laughed through the whole thing (and I'm a chick…LOL).

### Brian Olea, On-Air Personality, Mansion Mayhem, Playboy Radio, SiriusXM 102

I thought after 16 years working at the Playboy Mansion, I knew everything about women! Joe has definitely done his research and his book has even taught me a thing or two! Proof that not all women are alike!

### Tamazon, Night Owls Reviews (Top Pick)

Field Guide to Chicks of the United States by Joe Bovino is a hilarious look into the women of the USA. If you like people watching and commenting I can say you need to check this book out today. You and your friends will want to read this together for the most laughs.

### MAXIM Magazine

Outlandishly Hilarious.

### Concerned citizen (APO, AE USA) 5.0 out of 5 stars – Amazon.com

Great gift for ANYONE: Enjoyed the book so much I've been bought it for the embassy Marine guards here in Bangkok to help them 'transition' to the states. ANY guy is a rock star in Thailand, so I want them to have a tactical advantage. Great product Joe.

### Mike Cernovich, Author, Lawyer, and Free Speech Activist

This is hilarious!

### Jason Horton, the World's Only White Male Comedian

The book to end all books.

### Baniva *5.0 out of 5 stars – Amazon.com*

I'm gay and I love it!...It is painfully accurate as I was able to match up some characteristics of my girlfriends to their cartoon counterparts. It's the most genius thing ever. Loved it so much I bought another for a friend who I consider a connoisseur of the "female species"!

### Amar B. (Chicago, IL USA) *5.0 out of 5 stars – Amazon.com*

This could be considered be the greatest book ever written since the Kama Sutra. Buying this book would constitute the smartest book buying decision you have ever made.

### xtime Past *- 5.0 out of 5 stars, Amazon.com*

This is one badass book! This has heavy red pill material and every MGTOW/PUA should read this...Pure fun and extensive research occurred and undertaken to bring this material to a shining light...Reread: YES. RP/MGTOW: YES. [Rating:] 10/10. Thanks for adding smiles to our faces! Bravo!

### Mike B. "Cashcowz" *5.0 out of 5 stars – Amazon.com*

If there were a Pulitzer Prize for originality and humor, this book would be a slam dunk winner. Creative format, entertaining yet educational text, and fantastic illustrations are synthesized to perfection. Whether it's "How-to", "Has-been", or "Wish-I-could", this book is the bible for the Chickspotter in all of us - including females who should keep an eye on the competition.

### Tony Bruno, Sports Talk Radio Legend

My book finally got published!...Good job, Joe (Bovino). I couldn't resist picking it up in a men's store at MGM Grand in Vegas.

**Prince Billy Alexander III, Entertainment Investigative Field Producer, at Fox News, TMZ, and RADAR**

My new Bible.

**Braden Traub** *5.0 out of 5 stars – Amazon.com*

I'll be frank here — every American man should have this book proudly displayed on his coffee table. I know that I'll be handing out several of these this Christmas and I highly recommend everyone do the same. Do NOT miss this book.

**Rohit Bhargava** *@rohitbhargava*

Field Guide to Chicks is offensively brilliant.

# CHICASPOTTING

## A FIELD GUIDE TO LATINAS OF THE UNITED STATES

### JOE BOVINO

Three-Time #1 Bestselling Author

# NOTICE

Copyright © 2015 Joe Bovino
All rights reserved

No part of this book may be used or reproduced in any manner whatsoever without written permission from Joe Bovino, the author and founder of Bovino Law Group, P.A., or his designated representative, except in the case of brief quotations embodied in critical articles or reviews.

By purchasing and/or downloading this book, you acknowledge and agree to the following: You understand that the information in this book is an opinion and should be used for personal entertainment purposes only. You are responsible for your own behavior and nothing in this book is to be considered legal or personal advice with regard to any specific situation or problem.

You are entitled to one copy of this book for your personal use and enjoyment only. You do not have the right to sell, resell, distribute, copy, or otherwise use this book in any other way.

The author, publisher, and their representatives actively and regularly search the Internet for individuals who violate their copyrights, trademarks, and other intellectual property rights and take whatever action is necessary to enforce and protect them.

Please note that the legal penalties for copyright infringement alone include:

- \* Actual damages incurred by the copyright owner and any additional profits of the infringer;
- \* Statutory damages up to $150,000 per act of infringement;
- \* An injunction to stop the infringing acts; and
- \* Payment of all attorneys fees and costs by the infringing party.

"JOE BOVINO" and "CHICASPOTTING" are trademarks of Joe Bovino.

ISBN 978-0-9863326-6-1

**Note:** If you purchased and/or downloaded this book from a suspicious or seemingly unauthorized source, including but not limited to eBay, please report that site to info@bovinolawgroup.com. Thank you.

# DEDICATION

*To All The Chicas I've Loved Before*

# CONTENTS

**INTRODUCTION** .... 1
- Disclaimer .... 1
- Chicaspotting: Is It Really All About That Bass? .... 1
- How This Book Works .... 3
- How to Spot Chicas .... 7
- Parts of a Chica .... 9

**SPECIES PROFILES**
- Taco Belle (Mexican American) .... 12
- Bumbshell (Brazilian American) .... 16
- Euro-Mina (Argentine American) .... 20
- Symmetrical Force (Colombian American) .... 24
- Ecuadorable (Ecuadorian American) .... 28
- La Guitarra (Puerto Rican – South) .... 32
- Nuyorican (Puerto Rican – Northeast) .... 36
- Trifecta (Venezuelan American) .... 40
- Transformer (Cuban American) .... 44
- Perusian (Peruvian American) .... 48
- Cinnamon Swirl (Dominican American - Florida) .... 52
- Beauty Call (Dominican American – Northeast) .... 56
- Pupusa (Salvadoran American) .... 60
- Hotemalan (Guatemalan American) .... 64

| | | |
|---|---|---|
| *Conclusion* | .... | 69 |
| *About the Author* | .... | 70 |
| *Credits* | .... | 72 |
| *Notes* | .... | 73 |

# INTRODUCTION

"Why is the fact that each of us comes from a culture with its own distinctive mix of strengths and weaknesses, tendencies and predispositions, so difficult to acknowledge? Who we are cannot be separated from where we're from …"

—Malcolm Gladwell, *Outliers: The Story of Success*

## Disclaimer

Chicaspotting requires a sense of humor. So, if you're a sanctimonious dullard or cranky social justice warrior who's easily offended by colorful talk about women and ethnicity, put this book down, save your money, and go back to making the world a little less free and enjoyable for everyone else. This book is not intended for you.

## Chicaspotting: Is It Really All About That Bass?

In my first book, *Field Guide to Chicks of the United States*, I employed the techniques and methodology of arguably the best and most enthusiastic observers of nature in the American field — birders — to profile 90 subcultures (or "species") of American and hyphenated-American women. I called it "chickspotting," a variant of two of the world's most popular pastimes, bird watching and people watching.

An observation-based approach to the study of women, dating, and relationships made sense for three reasons. First, unlike most books and articles on the subject, mine stuck to the facts. Instead of trying to determine *why* women

behave as they do or look a certain way, it examined *what* they do and *how* to spot them when they do it. Second, by keeping it pithy, illustrated, and easy to read two pages at time (on the john), I stood a better chance of getting guys to read it, not just their wives and girlfriends. Third, I thought it was funny. If I couldn't write a book that was insightful *and* entertaining, I wasn't interested.

This book will apply the same techniques and methodology to the identification and analysis of one specific group of women— Latinas of the United States. Truth is, you can't fully understand and appreciate the allure of America's Latinas until you can distinguish between the species. Chickspotting, or in this case *"chicaspotting,"* will help you to do just that.

Some critics of my first book insist that every woman is unique (or the same) and any attempt to analyze or categorize women by group, culture, or ethnicity is sexist and wrong. Some assert that all such generalizations perpetuate harmful stereotypes. Others claim that words like "chicks," "chicas," and "species" objectify women, regardless of the context.

I don't see it that way. It's undeniably true that inner beauty is what really counts with people — unlike birds — but let's not put our heads in the sand. Anyone can see that the American field includes a wide variety of women from different ethnic and regional subcultures. Just look around.

Consider the Italian-American *Guidette*. Early drafts of my first book included a species profile of the *Guidette* long before MTV aired its "Jersey Shore" reality television series. She was relatively unknown back then. Now, almost everyone has too much information about the Guidette and her male counterpart, the Guido. Did MTV accomplish this by identifying a stereotype, a subculture, or both? That question led to big controversy and ratings, but one thing is clear: A *Guidette* subculture exists and many people find it fascinating ... in a train-wreck sort of way.

Cultural strengths, weaknesses, tendencies, and pre-dispositions, like distinctive physical traits, distinguish us from one another in meaningful

ways, and there's nothing wrong with acknowledging it. Moreover, as Samuel P. Huntington explained in *The Clash of Civilizations and the Remaking of World Order*, cultural identity matters. He put it this way:

> "In the post-Cold War world flags count and so do other symbols of cultural identity, including crosses, crescents, and even head coverings, because culture counts, and cultural identity is what is most meaningful to most people."

Latinas of the United States tend to identify strongly with their cultural background. You can see it in the way they look, talk, and act. And they'll tell you all about it if you ask them, as I did while conducting research for my books. Some even grouse about gringos who assume they're all the same and don't make a serious effort to understand their distinct culture and customs.

Well, if cultural identify matters so much to America's Latinas, shouldn't the rest of us take a little time to learn something about it? I think so, especially if we can have some fun in the process. Besides, it's not a selfless task. Increasing your cross-cultural IQ leads to all sorts of wonderful things, including new friends, dates, and girlfriends who were previously out of your comfort zone. Who knows? You may even find the love of your life.

## How This Book Works

### Species Profiles

Species profiles are the key to this guide. Each one includes several pages of full-color illustrations, charts, symbols, and maps. You can read them from front to back or move directly to the ones that interest you the most.

The Latin American species profiled in this guide are as follows:

1. Taco Belle (Mexican American);
2. Bumbshell (Brazilian American);
3. Euro-Mina (Argentine American);
4. Trifecta (Venezuelan American);
5. Symmetrical Force (Colombian American);
6. Transformer (Cuban American);
7. Ecuadorable (Ecuadorian American);
8. La Guitarra (Puerto Rican – South);
9. Nuyorican (Puerto Rican – Northeast);
10. Cinnamon Swirl (Dominican American – Florida);
11. Beauty Call (Dominican American – Northeast);
12. Perusian (Peruvian American);
13. Pupusa (Salvadoran American); and
14. Hotemalan (Guatemalan American).

## Species and Common Name

Each species name appears prominently at the top of the page, followed by the more common name associated with it.

This guide profiles species of Latinas who are present in significant numbers within the United States. However, due to the sheer number and diversity of Latinas in the country, it does not include profiles on some species with small representation (e.g., Panamanian American) or with marginal interest from men. An effort will be made to broaden coverage in subsequent editions.

## Illustrations

Full-page color illustrations of each species profiled in the guide create visual references to help you identify chicas in their natural environment.

## Appearance

The appearance section of each profile provides information on physical clues for identification of each Latin American species, including distinctive facial features, body parts, and skin tone. It also includes identifying information about her typical size, body type, penchant for cosmetic or plastic surgery (especially breast implants), and fashion sense.

## Behavior

This section deals with physical clues to identity as reflected in the behavior of the species. The anthropological findings in this section are primarily based on observable behavioral tendencies and related personality traits — not stereotypes, archetypes, or subjective opinions — but there's overlap at times. It's unavoidable.

Field data for this section was derived from many sources, including the author's personal experience, education, and training; relevant studies, books, magazines, and newspaper articles; online research; dating websites; and interviews with hundreds of male and female chicaspotters who were kind enough to answer probing questions on the subject.

Each profile also includes a behavioral trait chart and promiscuity zipper that rank the species as follows:

- **Friendliness** (with one smiley face as least friendly and five as most): Friendliness refers to how approachable and gregarious she is, how much she laughs and smiles, and how quickly she warms to strangers.

- **Neuroticism** (with one bloody cleaver as least neurotic and five as most): Neuroticism refers to how stressed out, anxious, or potentially psychotic she is or appears to be.

- **Nesting** (with one bird's nest as least interested in marriage and kids, and five as most): Nesting refers to how determined and likely she is to get married young, have kids, and settle down — but also reflects the priority that she tends to place on family, and how often she sacrifices career to be a homemaker or stay-at-home mom.

- **Maintenance** (with one hammer as lowest maintenance and five as highest): Maintenance refers to how much love, attention, and support she needs to feel satisfied in a relationship.

- **Superficiality** (with one bag of money as least superficial and five as most): Superficiality refers to how many purely superficial considerations (e.g., money, looks, or ethnicity) play into mate selection and serve as powerful chica magnets.

- **Promiscuity** (with one, zipped up , as least promiscuous and ten, unzipped, as most): Promiscuity refers to how likely she is to sleep around and have casual sex while single.

## How to Spot Chicas

Chicas at a bar or grocery store may hang around long enough for you to get a good look, but others pass by rapidly and don't give you much time to spot, identify, and (hopefully) meet them. Your job is to check them out as well as you can without staring, leering, or stalking, none of which are wise or recommended. Try to catch at least a glimpse of her face and body, listen carefully, and pay attention to how she acts before drawing any conclusions. If you focus on clues to identification noted in this guide, you'll do just fine.

Most chicaspotters already excel at noticing T&A, and sometimes that's all the information you need to identify a particular species, but don't stop there. Learn to spot less obvious field marks. You'll make lots of mistakes, but practice makes perfect, as they say. Plus, Latinas of the United States almost always appreciate gringos who try to understand the physical and cultural differences between them.

## Cross-Referencing

Many Latinas of the United States identify with more than one ethnic or regional subculture. These "multi-species" chicas can be hard to spot, but that's no reason to throw in the towel. In most cases, a little cross-referencing between species profiles will do the trick, especially if you're familiar with all 90 species of American and hyphenated-American women profiled in my first book, *Field Guide to Chicks of the United States*.

Here's the bottom line: When you encounter a chica who doesn't fit neatly into one or more species profiles, get creative. Apply information from as many profiles as it takes to better identify, understand, and interact with her in the field. Refresh your recollection by quickly browsing through relevant profiles (on your smart phone), if necessary. You can even use the field guide itself as an ice-breaker at times. If nothing else, she'll remember you.

And, for God's sake, ask questions!

Chicas, unlike birds, can tell you all you need to know.

Last but not least, don't worry about guessing wrong or striking out occasionally. This is chicaspotting, not a bombing mission over 'Nam. If you relax, laugh at your mistakes, and modify your approach on the fly, you'll enjoy chicaspotting more and gradually improve your recognition, understanding and — most importantly — *appreciation* of America's Latinas … even if you miss the mark on a regular basis.

It happens to the best of us.

Okay, that's all I have to say about that.

**Now, let's go chicaspotting.**

# Parts of a Chica

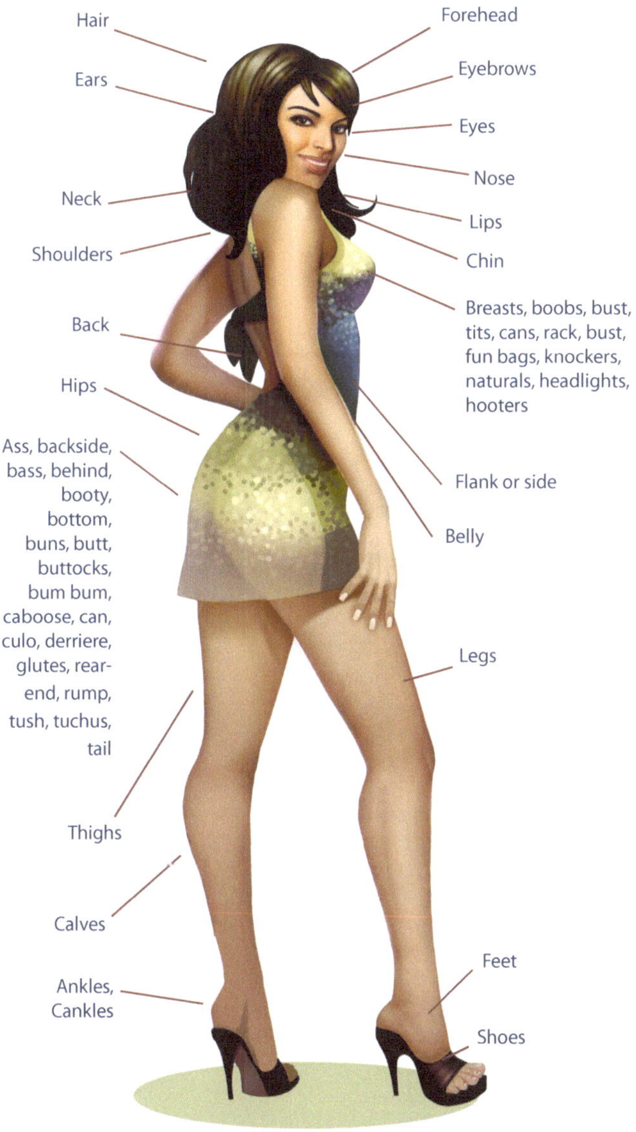

- Hair
- Ears
- Neck
- Shoulders
- Back
- Hips
- Ass, backside, bass, behind, booty, bottom, buns, butt, buttocks, bum bum, caboose, can, culo, derriere, glutes, rear-end, rump, tush, tuchus, tail
- Thighs
- Calves
- Ankles, Cankles
- Forehead
- Eyebrows
- Eyes
- Nose
- Lips
- Chin
- Breasts, boobs, bust, tits, cans, rack, bust, fun bags, knockers, naturals, headlights, hooters
- Flank or side
- Belly
- Legs
- Feet
- Shoes

# Optional Enhancements

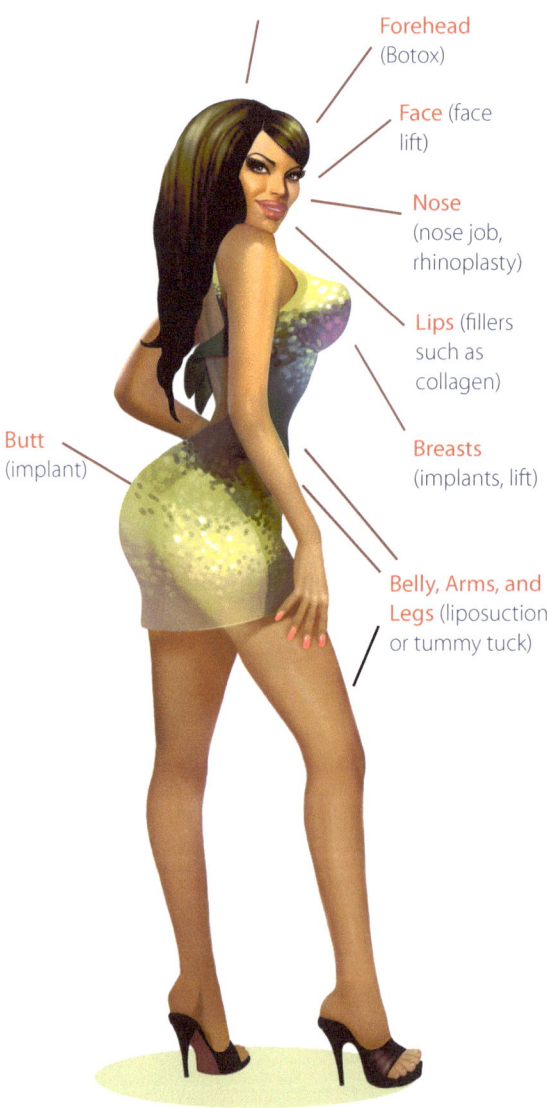

Hair (extensions, coloring, curling, straightening, highlights)

Forehead (Botox)

Face (face lift)

Nose (nose job, rhinoplasty)

Lips (fillers such as collagen)

Breasts (implants, lift)

Belly, Arms, and Legs (liposuction or tummy tuck)

Butt (implant)

# TACO BELLE™
## (Mexican American)

CHICASPOTTING

JOE BOVINO

**APPEARANCE:** This chica — not to be confused with Taco Bell® fast food — is recognizable by her dusky complexion with heavy makeup, brown hair, brown eyes, and facial features that reveal Native American ancestry. Normally curvy and petite or medium-sized, with large or medium-sized breasts and a wide butt that's flat at the top and round at the bottom. Often out of shape because exercise is less emphasized in Mexican culture, but wears very tight jeans and shirts with a bare midriff to show off her figure anyway. Rarely wears unflattering gym clothes in public or gets tattoos, which are still considered trashy in Mexico.

## NOTABLES

Raquel Pomplun, Yanet Garcia (not American, but wow), Eva Longoria, Thalia, Elsa Benitez, Mia St. John, Erika Medina, Pennelope Jimenez, and Cierra Ramirez.

## TO HAVE AND TO HOLD

Sara Ramirez, a curvy, size 14 (at best) Taco Belle actress known for her role on the *Grey's Anatomy* TV show, summed up one of the benefits of her extra pounds this way: "I know my boyfriend loves to have something to hold on to. There are a lot of men out there who do." That's true, but stunning Raquel Pomplun shows how hot a Taco Belle can be if she exercises regularly.

**BEHAVIOR:** Warm and cuddly as a teddy bear but (somewhat) shy around strangers, especially gringos. Values Mexican culture, with its focus on family, religion (mainly Catholic), love, and tradition. Normally hardworking but not particularly ambitious or well-educated because she doesn't want career to interfere with family. This generation is far more driven and independent, however. Frequently works in a (blue-collar) service industry or as a skilled artisan. Loves dancing, music, food, and family gatherings.

**SONG:** Generally soft-spoken but much louder in her comfort zone with friends and family. Uses exaggerated tones and gestures to convey passion and a sense of drama, as you can plainly see on any Mexican soap opera. Often prefers to speak Spanish as much as possible.

## DON'T BE SO SARCASTIC

Sarcasm is considered disrespectful in Mexican culture and doesn't translate well into Spanish.

**MATING:** Highly feminine but demands respect. Often (somewhat) dependent on her man. Exceptionally sentimental, attentive, and nurturing but melodramatic and smothering at times. Seductive and sensual but reluctant to have sex before a level of trust has been established, unless she's relatively young and rebellious. Occasionally sleeps with white guys sooner than usual because they're perceived as less judgmental than Mexican men, and her Catholic sense of shame has faded considerably in recent years. Known to wait three dates to two months (or more) before closing the deal.

**MAGNETS:** Attracted to Latin (primarily Mexican) and white gentlemen who are respectful, family-oriented, and capable of making her feel safe and secure. Seldom a gold digger but expects to be supported financially and emotionally. Often drawn to significantly older men because age isn't a big deal in Mexican culture and is associated with many positive qualities. Guys who speak Spanish or show a genuine interest in her culture also have a big edge. Rarely attracted to "bad boys" unless she's lower-class and/or doesn't identify with Mexican culture much anymore.

## BEING OLDER CAN WORK IN YOUR FAVOR

Most American women aren't interested in considerably older men unless they're wealthy and, ahem, generous. Not so the Taco Belle. She's often physically attracted to much older men for cultural reasons having little or nothing to do with money.

**HABITAT:** Mexican party or nightclub; soccer game; Catholic Church; Latin music concert.

**LOCATION:** Abundant in Texas, especially San Elizario, Tornillo, Lopezville, Progreso, Cameron Park, Presidio, Alton, Hidalgo, Cactus, Penitas, Palmview, Roma, Fort Hancock, Heidelberg, San Juan, and La Joya; California, especially Calexico, Coachella, Huron, Parlier, Lost Hills, Mecca, East Los Angeles, and San Joaquin; and Arizona, especially Somerton and Nogales. Abundant to somewhat common in parts of Washington, New Mexico, Nevada, Idaho, Illinois, Florida, Utah, and Colorado.

**MIGRATION:** Migratory.

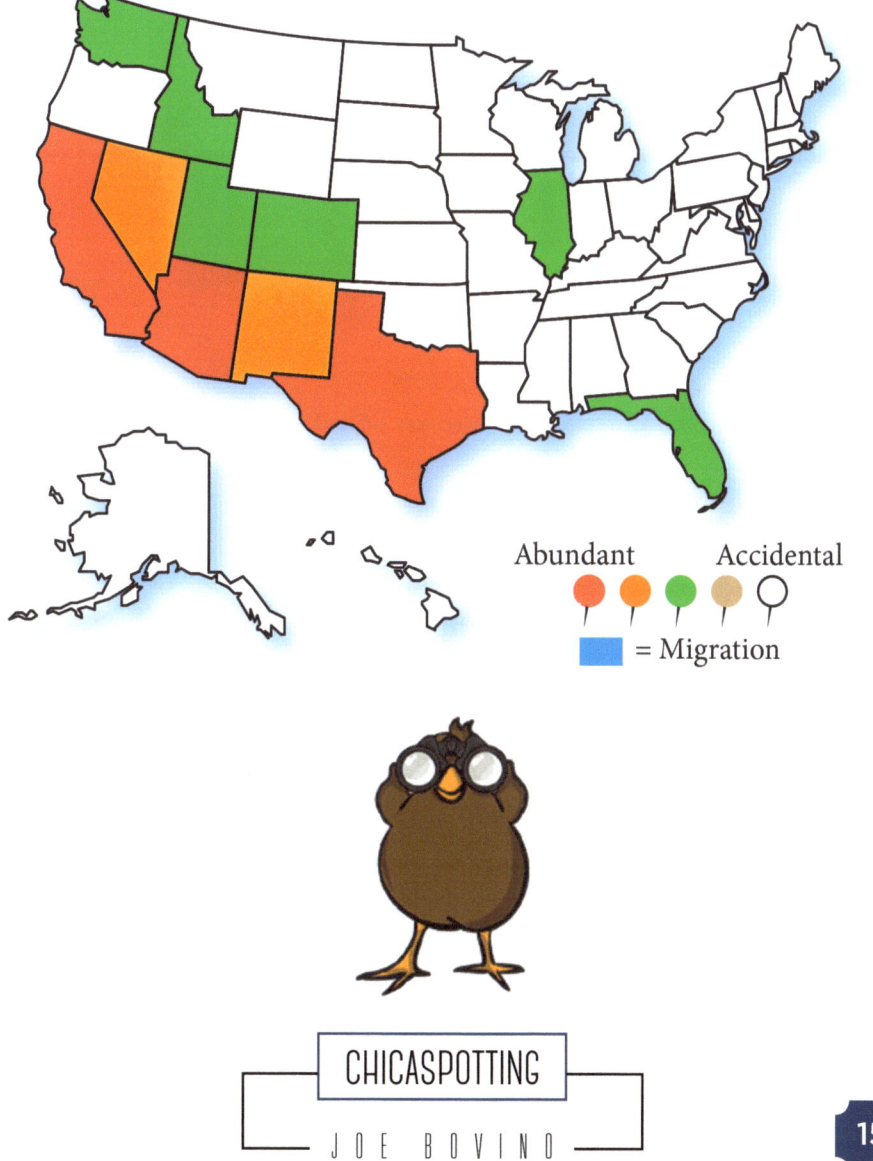

CHICASPOTTING

JOE BOVINO

# BUMBSHELL™
(Brazilian American)

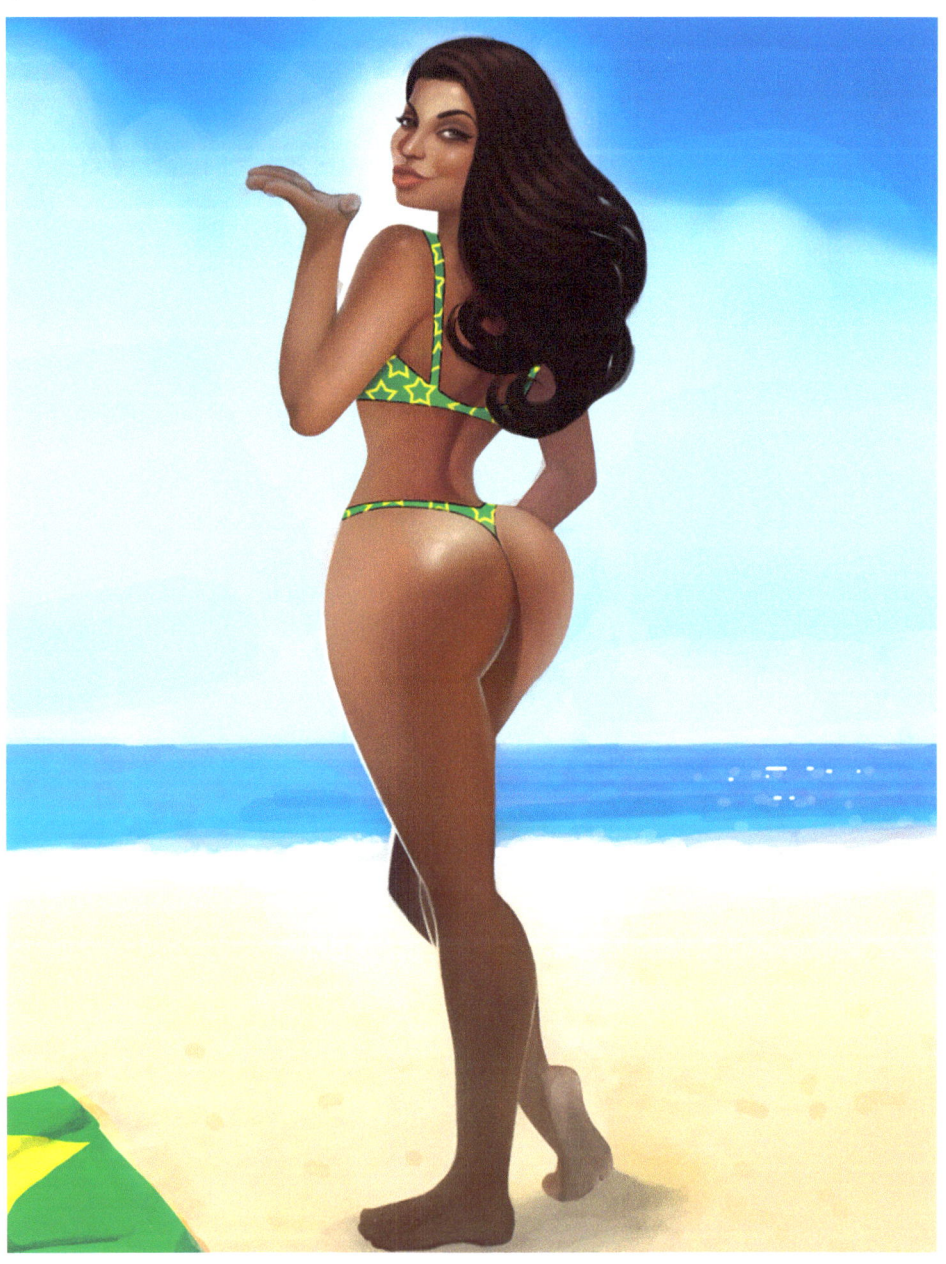

**APPEARANCE:** Ask this happy-go-lucky chica about her best feature and chances are she'll turn around and show you her big, cheeky bum bum. Other field marks include strong, sexy legs; a small waist; naturally small breasts (but boob jobs are increasingly common); a lean, athletic frame; twinkling brown eyes; full lips; and a warm smile. Often a curly or wavy-haired brunette with optional highlights. Complexion varies from golden to dark brown. Dresses to be sexy and loves to wear a skimpy Brazilian bikini with optional anklet.

## NOTABLES

Adriana Lima, Camila Alves-McConaughey, Alessandra Ambrosia, Isabeli Fontana, Gisele Bundchen, Alice Braga, Gleicy Santos, and Morena Baccarin.

**BEHAVIOR:** Exceptionally upbeat, sociable, and non-confrontational. Rarely loses her sense of humor or takes life too seriously. Spontaneous and adventurous but seldom punctual. Social life revolves around family and friends, not work. Often religious (Roman Catholic and Protestant) and interested in astrology, psychic readings, or other mystic pursuits.

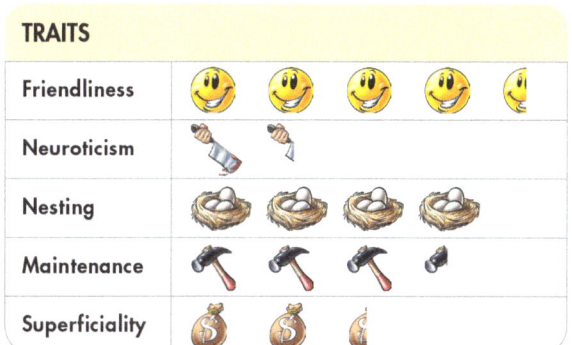
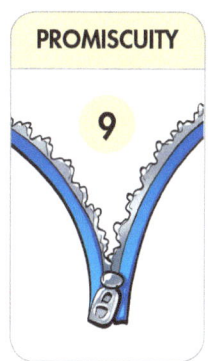

**SONG:** Enjoys small talk, laughter, and displays of affection as means of communication. Occasionally loud. Brazilian Portuguese, not Spanish, is her native tongue. Normally doesn't even like the sound of Spanish. Known to baffle gringos because "Yes" (Sim) means anything from "Yes" to "Perhaps" to "No;" "Perhaps" (Talvez) means "No;" "No" (Não) means "Absolutely never. Not in a million years. This is the craziest thing I've ever been asked;" "A hug! A kiss!" (Um abraço! Um beijo!) means "Take care. Bye;" "Let's see" (Vamos ver) means "Not a chance. Please drop it;" and "I'll be there in ten minutes" (Vou chegar em dez minutinhos) means "Sometime in the next half-hour I'll get up off the sofa and start looking for my keys."

**MATING:** Arguably the most promiscuous of America's Latinas, despite her Christian faith. Loves foreplay, especially kissing. Always fully waxed and ready for action. Highly flirtatious, sensual, and sexually uninhibited but often scandalous and fickle. Typically expects a guy to assume a portion of her extended family's financial obligations in Brazil if the relationship gets serious. Known to wait one to four dates (more or less) before closing the deal.

## A KISS IS JUST A KISS

Don't be surprised if the Bumbshell kisses you lustfully in one moment and someone else the same way in the next. She loves to kiss but makes a clear distinction between kissing (which commonly happens fast) and everything else (which normally requires an investment of some time and energy). She may also lie (to spare your feelings), cheat (to indulge her own), and/or keep ex-boyfriends around (just in case).

**MAGNETS:** Attracted to men who are successful, generous (with their money, time, and love), family-oriented, and patient when she acts in ways they don't understand. The hotter she is, the more likely she is to be attracted only to rich guys. Tends to assume that white men have money, but may also assume that they're relatively boring (by Brazilian standards), anal-retentive, and uncoordinated (on the dance floor).

## UP CLOSE AND PERSONAL

Unlike most American women, the Bumbshell doesn't require much personal space to feel comfortable and is easily approachable. In fact, guys who maintain a safe, respectful, Anglo-Saxon distance risk blowing it when she incorrectly assumes that they're uninterested or gay. She also tends to think that the American accent is sexy, *especially when spoken softly into her ear*. So move in, fellas. And *stay close*. A kiss - or more - may await you.

**HABITAT:** Beach; pool; boat/yacht; beauty/nail salon; gym; health food store; mall; Catholic church; (Brazilian) restaurant; concert; art exhibit; popular lounge or nightclub (with dancing); cool sports bar; private party.

**LOCATION:** Somewhat common to casual in New Jersey (especially East Newark, Harrison, Long Branch, and Kearny); south Florida (especially North Bay Village, Bay Harbor Islands, Miami Beach, North Miami Beach, Surfside, Key Biscayne, Aventura, Doral, Deerfield Beach, Pompano Beach, Oakland Park, and Lighthouse Point); Massachusetts (especially Framingham, Vineyard Haven, Marlborough, and Everett); Danbury, CT; Los Angeles County (especially Redondo Beach and Venice Boulevard in West LA); and "Little Brazil" in NYC.

**MIGRATION:** Migratory.

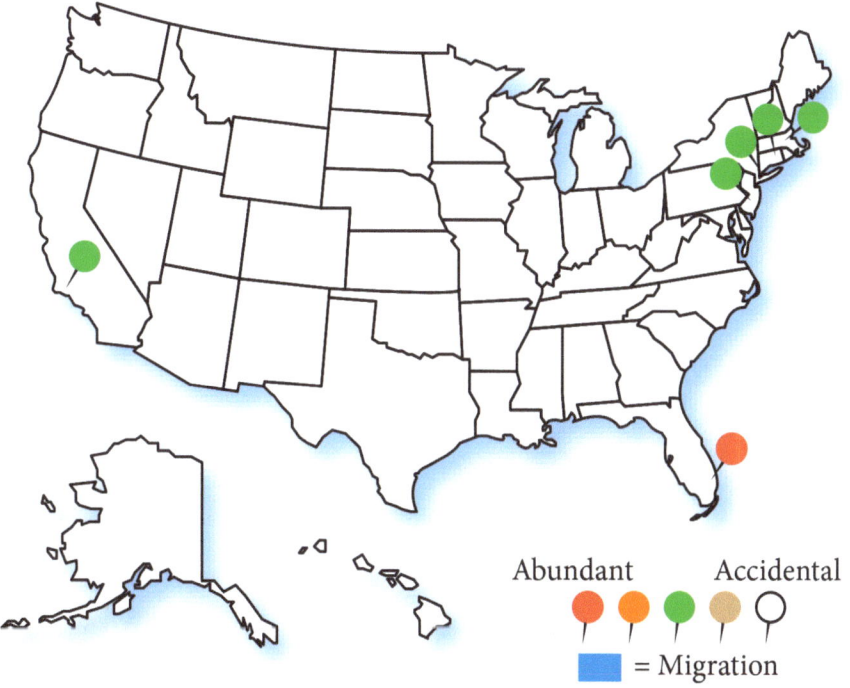

# EURO-MINA™
## (Argentine American)

CHICASPOTTING — JOE BOVINO

**APPEARANCE:** The Euro-Mina tends to look more Italian or Spanish than Latin and dresses with a French flair for fashion. (About 90% of Argentines are immigrants from Italy and Spain and their descendants.) Almost always slender — Argentina has one of the highest rates of anorexia — with a petite frame and small bone structure, but still somewhat shapely, although not in a Barbie doll way. Less likely to supersize a boob job or wear heavy makeup than other Latinas. Often has straight, dark hair (although a minority are naturally or artificially blond), fair to light brown skin, and striking (dark) eyes.

## NOTABLES

Pampita Ardohain, Valeria Mazza, Marianela Pereyra, Yamila Díaz-Rahi (aka Yamila Diaz), Luján Fernández, Inés Rivero, Luciana Scarabello, Inés Rivero, and Julie Gonzalo.

**BEHAVIOR:** Warm and friendly around people she likes but occasionally snobbish, condescending, and dismissive to others, especially blacks, Asians, and non-Argentines. Family-oriented, emotional, and passionate but in more of a Southern European than Latin way. Outgoing, proud, and confident but realistic and aware of her own shortcomings. Relatively well-educated and industrious. Loves dancing (especially the tango), music, and the outdoors. Predominantly Roman Catholic but, like many Europeans, rarely goes to church.

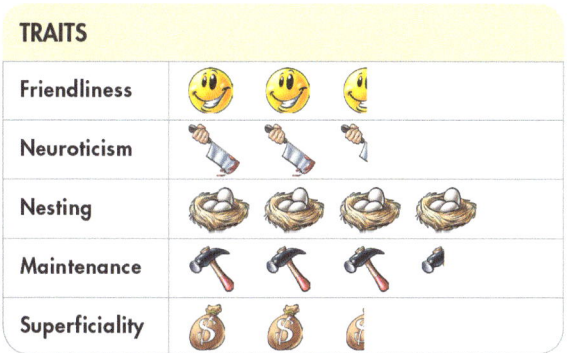
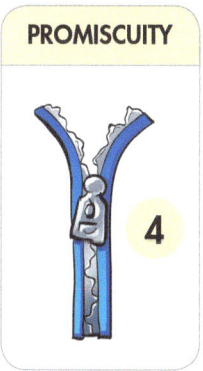

**SONG:** Expresses her opinions in a direct and open way. Says and does whatever it takes to get her point across. Doesn't hesitate to criticize others, raise her voice, curse, or point out how others (without her Southern European ancestry) are less cultured.

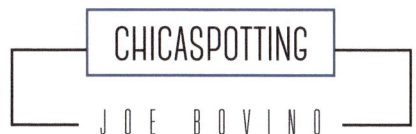

## NO PATIENCE FOR POLITICAL CORRECTNESS

The Euro-Mina has something to say, a right to say it, and no patience for political correctness. If you can't handle it, it's your problem, not hers.

**MATING:** Enjoys little dating games and playing hard to get, unlike many Latinas. Amorous but seldom sleeps with a guy on the first date and isn't particularly interested in casual sex. Frequently a bit demanding, possessive, jealous, and territorial, however. Moody or whiny too at times. Known to wait three weeks to two months before closing the deal.

## KEEP HER GUESSING

The Euro-Mina needs a challenge and doesn't mind taking on a player or bad boy. She can handle whoever comes her way in stride. So be strong in your pursuit but inject a little uncertainty about your level of interest.

**MAGNETS:** Traditionally attracted to real men ("machistas") with strong personalities who are self-assured, charismatic, and charming, but increasingly tired of the extreme, stereotypical version. Normally goes for white or Latin guys but occasionally dates other types with lots of personality, intelligence, and/or money.

## NO BETA MALES

Always approach the Euro-Mina self-assuredly. She may even overlook the fact that you're not particularly good-looking if you don't seem intimidated. Fearlessness — real or feigned — is sexy.

**HABITAT:** City restaurant; café; shopping mall; polo match; park; lounge or nightclub (with dancing); party; beach.

**LOCATION:** Somewhat common in Miami Beach, Sunny Isles Beach, Plantation Mobile Home Park, Bay Harbor Islands, North Bay Village, Key Biscayne, Surfside, Lauderdale-by-the-Sea, The Crossings, Ojus, Doral, and Aventura, FL; Deer Park, Acton, and East Richmond Heights, CA; Harbor Hills, Islandia, and Thomaston, NY; Lebanon, IL; and Mayland-Pleasant Hill, TN. Casual to accidental in other metropolitan areas of South Florida; New York City; Houston and Dallas, TX; California, Illinois, New York, New Jersey, Connecticut, and Western Pennsylvania.

**MIGRATION:** Migratory.

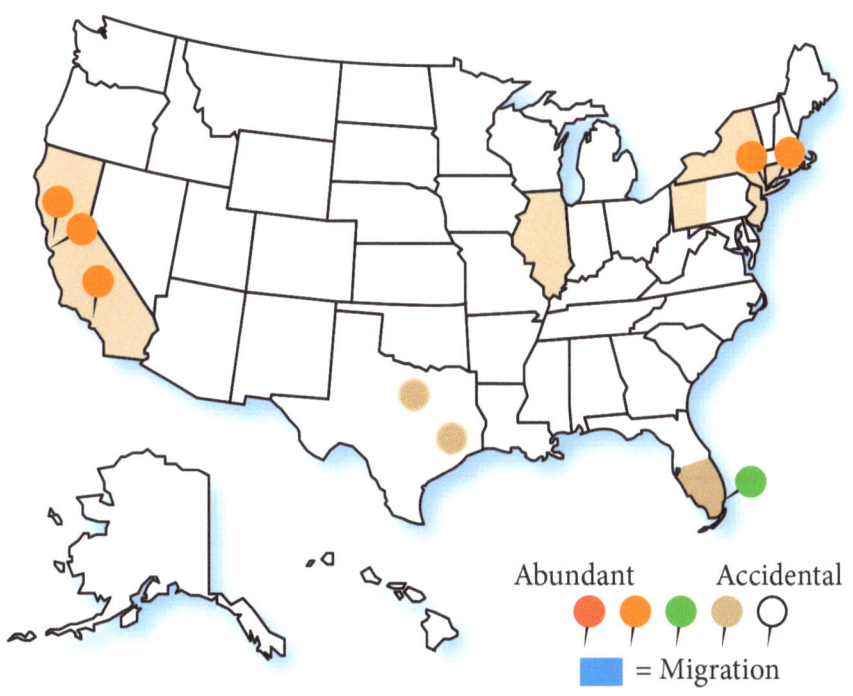

# SYMMETRICAL FORCE™
(Colombian American)

CHICASPOTTING

JOE BOVINO

**APPEARANCE:** Look for delicate, symmetrical features on a round, cute-as-a-button face; a big smile; long, dark brown or black hair that's silky smooth and straight or slightly wavy; wide-set brown eyes (often with a slight slant or bronze circles underneath); and soft bronzed or brown skin. Normally petite, finely-toned, and symmetrically shaped. Bust size varies, but breast implants are practically a rite of passage and she likes 'em **BIG**. Tends to seek aesthetic perfection through a nose job, liposuction, butt implants, or collagen injections. Impeccably well groomed, made-up, and maintained. Over-accessorizes with big belts, earrings, and the whole nine yards. Unafraid to wear white pants.

### NOTABLES

Sophia Vergara, Manuela Arbeláez (*The Price is Right*), Monica Fonseca, Paola Turbay (of Lebanese descent), Daniela Lopez Osorio, Paula Garces, Maria Checa, Karen Carreno, Lina Maya, Evelin Santos, Cindy Luna, Alba Galindo, and Ximena Duque.

**BEHAVIOR:** Exceptionally charming and gregarious but worldly, shrewd, and mysterious. Family-oriented, proud, and somewhat religious (mainly Roman Catholic) but intense, materialistic, and deeply cynical, especially about men. Surprisingly bright and entrepreneurial, but more likely to pursue a shortcut to success and the easiest way to get what she wants. Often places a higher priority on partying and dating than working or studying. Dances merengue, vallenato, cumbia, or salsa beautifully without any music. Easily annoyed if mistaken for another Latin American species, especially the *Taco Belle*.

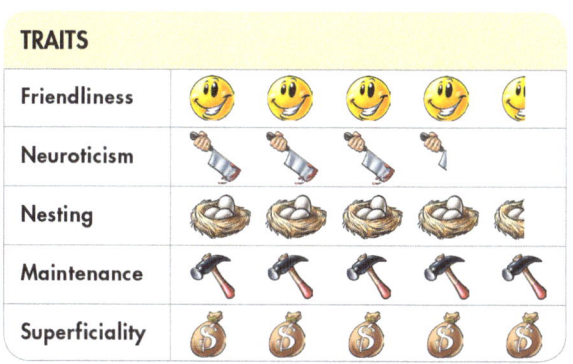

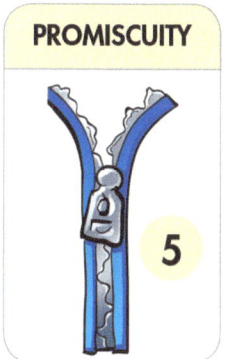

## WATCH YOUR BACK

Many Latinas secretly fear the Symmetrical Force because they know what a smooth and cunning operator lies beneath the sugary-sweet demeanor. They don't buy the whole nice-girl routine. Some of this anxiety comes from jealousy and possessiveness, but most comes from experience. So watch your back while you're watching hers.

**SONG:** Chatty and demonstrative, especially in singsong Spanish. Loves to laugh but loud and excitable at times. Often refers to all whites as "gringos" and all Asians as "Chinese." Common expressions include "Regalamelo." (Give it to me as a gift.)

**MATING:** Tries to be loyal but assumes that you'll cheat from day one and may beat you to the punch. Exceptional beauty coupled with an intense desire for comfort and security often translate into at least some measure of (direct or indirect) gold digging, game-playing, and/or visa-hunting. Sensual and attentive but exhausting at times. Known to wait two weeks to two months before closing the deal but expedites the process for rich guys.

**MAGNETS:** Attracted mainly to Latin, white, or Middle Eastern guys who are financially secure (because men are providers in her culture), generous (with their money), family-oriented, and convivial. It also helps to be well-mannered, clean — she's meticulous about cleanliness and odors — and Catholic.

## GIFTS AND CALLS

Arguably the most materialistic of America's Latinas, the Symmetrical Force isn't embarrassed or ashamed about a little gold digging, but thoughtful gifts (e.g., books or flowers) go a long way. She also expects you to call the day after a kiss and will hold it against you forever if you don't. Just sending a text usually won't cut it.

**HABITAT:** Beauty salon; gym; beach; pool; mall; trendy boutique; restaurant or bar; dance club; (exclusive) party; boat; church; (Latin music) concert; sporting event; red-carpet affair.

**LOCATION:** Common to somewhat common in New Jersey (especially Victory Gardens, Dover, Morristown, Englewood, West New York, and North Bergen); south Florida, with high concentrations in Miami (especially the booming Brickell financial district) and its suburbs (especially Doral, Kendall, and Hialeah), Country Club, Virginia Gardens, Key Biscayne, Kendale Lakes, Weston, and Sunny Isles Beach; Central Falls, RI; and parts of New York City (especially Queens, Montauk, Jackson Heights, and East Hampton North.

**MIGRATION:** Migratory.

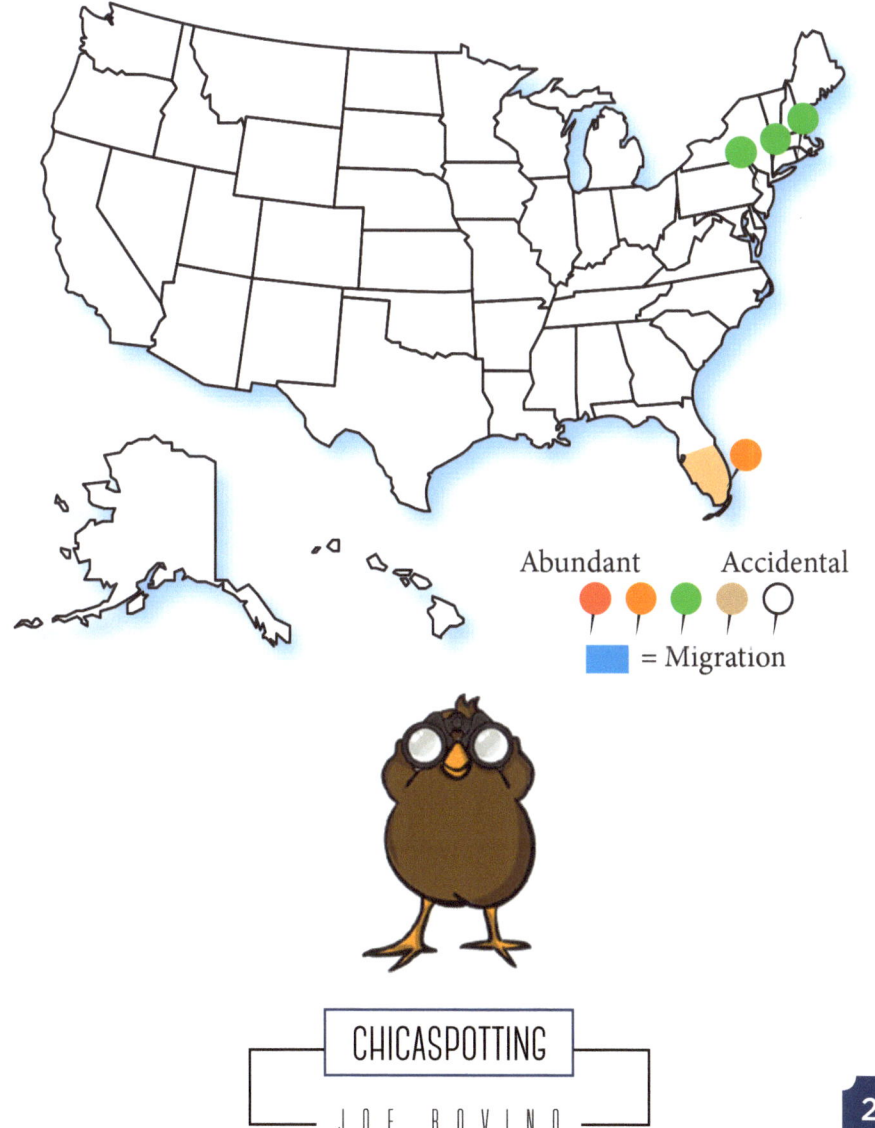

# ECUADORABLE™
(Ecuadorian American)

**APPEARANCE:** This diamond in the rough is a mix of Spanish, Indian, and/or African ancestry. She tends to be unusually skinny for a Latina — except for the even thinner and lighter-skinned *Euro-Mina* from Argentina — but manages to maintain her curves and shapely figure anyway. Other field marks include delicate facial features (including a tiny nose) on a small face, and straight, black (or colored) hair. Almost always tanned, well-groomed, stylishly dressed, and petite to medium height. Eye color varies.

**BEHAVIOR:** Tends to be outgoing, energetic, and happy-go-lucky but quite stubborn and aloof. Courteous, religious (Catholic), and "old-school" traditional in many ways but gets lost in her own world once in a while. Often bright, independent, and entrepreneurial without losing focus on the family. Loves to dance (merengue and salsa), cook, travel, and meet people of different ethnicities and cultures.

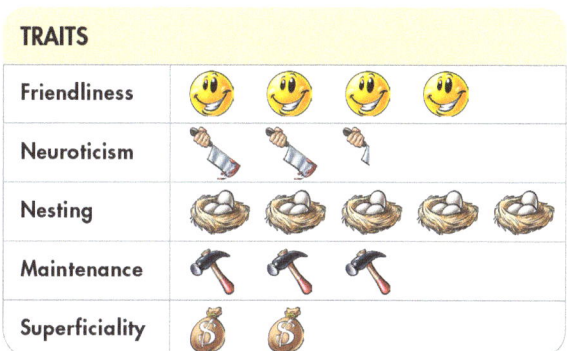 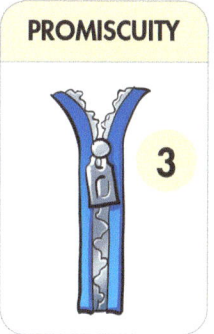

**SONG:** Outspoken, talkative, hard-headed (in fights), and slow to admit when she's wrong. Loud at times.

## ESTABLISH THE GROUND RULES

If your intentions aren't genuine or all you want is casual sex, tell her the truth up front. You may not get laid, but she won't hold it against you either.

**MATING:** Family-oriented but tends to call the shots in hers, one way or another. Horny and sexually adventurous but not easily taken to bed. (Well worth the wait, however). Demands attention, commitment, and plenty of sex in a relationship but wants you to be just as satisfied. Rarely hot-tempered unless she discovers that you're a serial liar or complete fraud, in which case you should run for the hills. Reliably loving, faithful, and loyal, but don't push her buttons. Known to wait one or two months before closing the deal.

**MAGNETS:** Attracted to men with similar views about family and career who take the lead, make her feel protected, and express a sincere interest in settling down. Usually dates Latin, white, or Middle Eastern guys.

**HABITAT:** Beach; pool; dance club; (karaoke) bar; café or lounge; (business) networking event; family gathering; private party with close friends.

**LOCATION:** Somewhat common to casual in New York, especially Sleepy Hollow, Montauk, Patchogue, Ossining, Port Chester, Springs, Peekskill, East Hampton, and New York City (mainly Jackson Heights, Brooklyn, and the Bronx); New Jersey, especially East Newark, Hightstown, Union City, Hackensack, West New York, North Bergen, Harrison, Guttenberg, East Windsor, Dover, Belleville, Jersey City, Union City, and Plainfield; Florida (especially Miami, Orlando, and Fort Lauderdale); and Danbury, Connecticut. Casual in Chicago, IL, Minneapolis, MN, and Los Angeles, CA.

**MIGRATION:** Migratory.

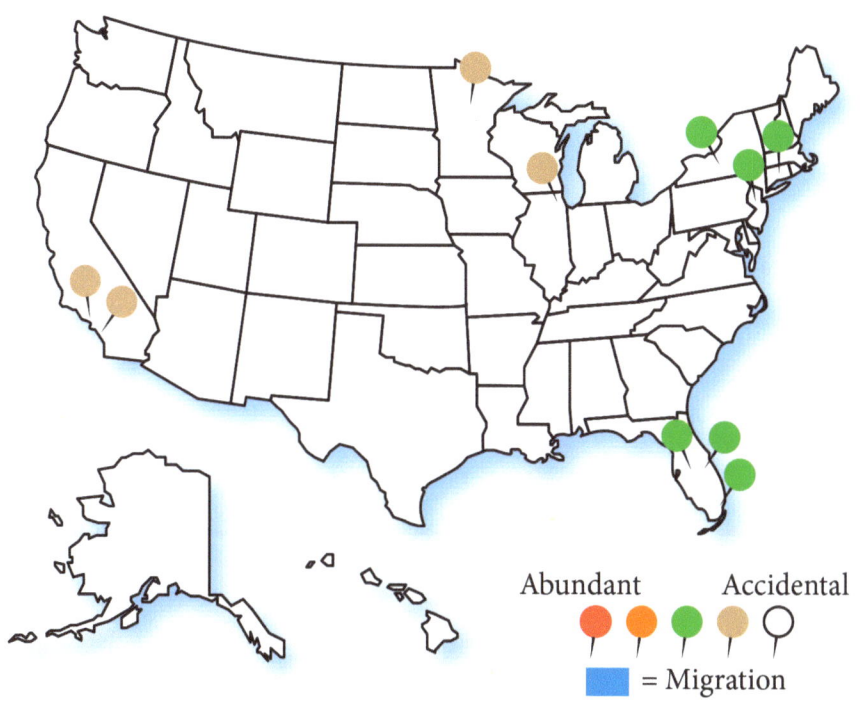

Abundant　　Accidental

= Migration

CHICASPOTTING

JOE BOVINO

# LA GUITARRA™
## (Puerto Rican – South)

**APPEARANCE:** This dangerously curvy chica, also known as "Mami Boricua" or "Boricua Mami," is recognizable by her guitar-shaped body, with a thick, shapely butt — similar to the leaner version of the Cuban American *Transformer* and a little thicker than a Brazilian American *Bumbshell* — tiny waist, and naturally small to medium-sized breasts. Often gets a boob job to balance things out. Normally petite to medium-height with distinctively golden brown skin derived from a mixture of Spanish and African ancestry, also known as "mancha de platano" (plantain-banana stain), sexy brown eyes, and long, dark brown hair. Commonly wears sexy, colorfully stylish clothing and accessories.

## NOTABLES

Roselyn Sánchez, Zuleyka Rivera, Victoria Justice (1/2 white), Joyce Giraud, Jaslene Gonzalez, and Gina Rodriquez (possibly *Nuyorican* or *La Guitarra/Nuyorican*).

## SHE'S NO VISA-HUNTER

Unlike many Latinas in the United States these days, La Guitarra doesn't need to marry you to get a green card. She's already a U.S. citizen.

**BEHAVIOR:** Devoted to family and faith (mainly Catholic). Proud to be Puerto Rican but with something to prove in the USA. Well-assimilated with other Latinos in Miami, Orlando, and other US cities outside the Northeast. Normally affable, gregarious, and bright but (somewhat) ostentatious. Usually smart, responsible, and sympathetic. Rarely associates with the *Nuyorican* (her Puerto Rican counterpart in New York and other parts of the Northeast) because of vast cultural differences between them. Loves to cook and dances remarkably well.

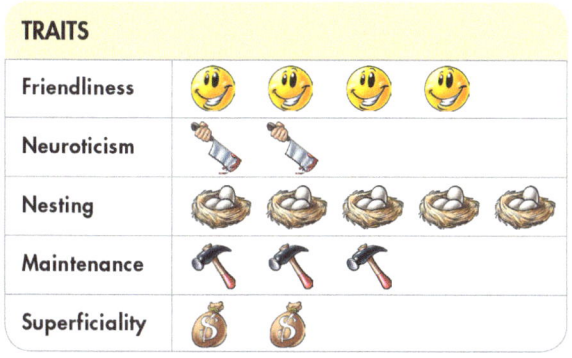
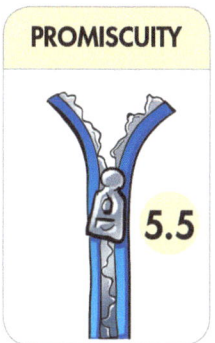

**SONG:** Talks quickly, laughs frequently, and loves to gesture with her hands. Multi-lingual but often prefers Spanish to English.

**MATING:** Feels pressure to remain a virgin or at least sustain the illusion until she ties the knot, which usually happens before she turns 25. Stops working after marriage to be a full-time housewife because family is her highest priority. Nurturing, considerate, and passionate but temperamental, jealous, and extremely territorial. Generally loyal but won't tolerate bad behavior indefinitely. Known to wait three weeks to two months before closing the deal.

### EAT YOUR WHEATIES

Expect La Guitarra to want sex as much or more than you do, no matter how hot she is. And not just in bed at night. She'll come at you in the shower, the kitchen, the closet, the garage, and just about anywhere else. Be ready to go at all times.

**MAGNETS:** Attracted mainly to Latin guys but occasionally dates white and Middle Eastern ones with similar values and behavioral tendencies. Seldom branches out from there.

**HABITAT:** Nail salon; beach; dance club; restaurant or bar; Catholic Church; private party with close friends and family; airport (especially MIA).

**LOCATION:** Common to somewhat common in Florida, especially Miami Gardens and elsewhere in Miami-Dade County, Yeehaw Junction, Poinciana, Azalea Park, Kissimmee, Interlachen, Union Park, and Buenaventura Lakes. Somewhat common in Orlando and Tampa, FL. Casual to accidental in other parts of the country, especially Chicago, Philadelphia, Cleveland, and parts of North Carolina, Virginia, Maryland, Massachusetts, and New Jersey.

**MIGRATION:** Migratory (mostly between the continental US and Puerto Rico).

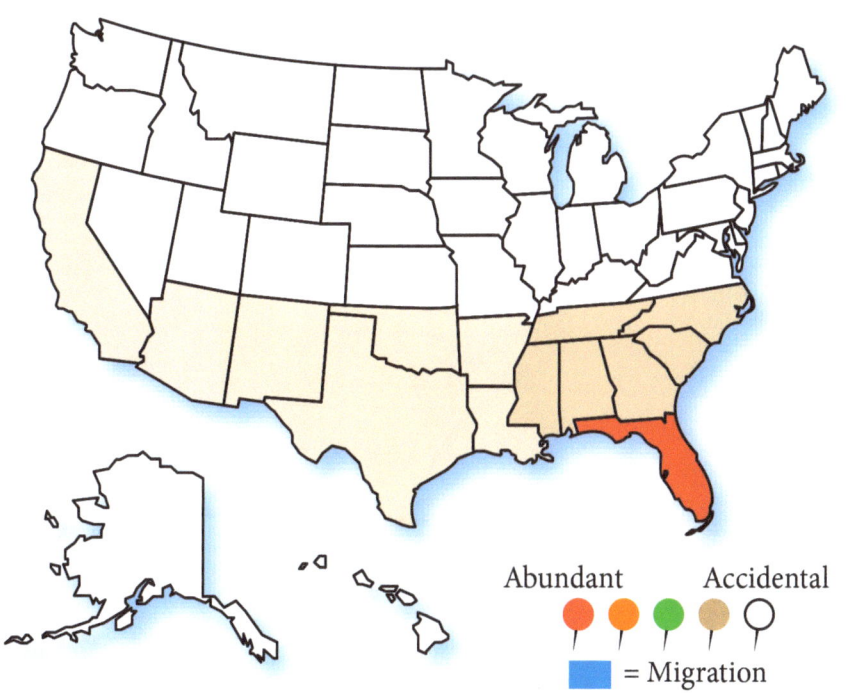

Abundant　　Accidental

= Migration

CHICASPOTTING

JOE BOVINO

# NUYORICAN™
## (Puerto Rican – Northeast)

**APPEARANCE:** The Nuyorican [noo-yor-ree-kan], also known as the "Ledge" or the "Shelf," tends to have an urban or ghetto-urban style due to extensive intermingling of Latin and black cultures in the region, but she glams it up at times. Look for a big, protruding butt, with naturally small to medium-sized breasts, golden brown skin, a prominent forehead, beautiful brown eyes, and long, dark brown hair. Often petite to medium-height. Breast implants are not the norm but increasingly common.

## TWO POTATOES ON STICKS

Jennifer Lopez is America's most famous Nuyorican. She put it this way: "As a Latin woman in the United States, you're taught that you should be skinnier, that you shouldn't have such a big butt. You feel self-conscious. I did. I was really thin, but I had a booty on me that you would not believe, like two potatoes on sticks." There was, however, a fringe benefit: "I could serve coffee using my rear as a ledge."

## NOTABLES

Rosario Dawson (1/2 NYC *So Ho'*), Jessica Caban (model girlfriend of Bruno Mars), Rosie Perez, Adrienne Bailon (1/2 *Ecuadorable*), LaLa Anthony, Jennifer Lopez, Talisa Soto, and Gina Rodriquez (possibly *La Guitarra/Nuyorican*).

**BEHAVIOR:** Family-oriented and spirited but not particularly friendly to strangers and occasionally (somewhat) aggressive. Often relatively uneducated and poor — with a poverty rate similar to the African-American *Bronx Tail* — but animated and passionate about life. Usually loves urban and Latin music (including lots of reggaeton), watching the "novelas," dancing, and singing.

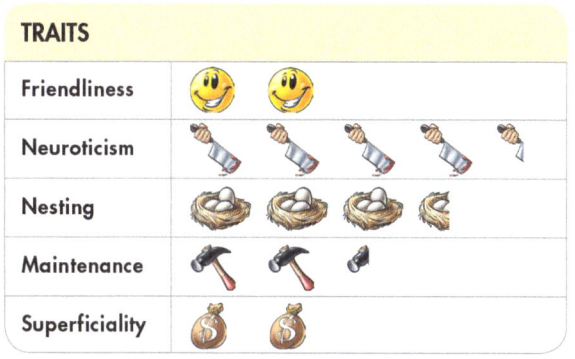
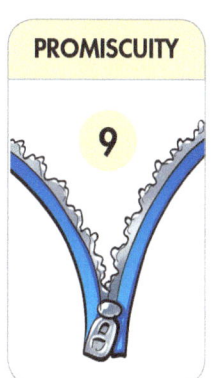

## DUAL IDENTITY

The Nuyorican has a dual identity (crisis) because she shares cultural traits with fully assimilated American blacks in the Northeast that differ greatly from the *La Guitarra* in South Florida and Puerto Rico.

**SONG:** Talks quickly and loudly. Tends to curse, use urban slang, say "culo" (ass) and "Que carajo!" (What the f*ck!), mangle grammar, and gesture dramatically. Often refers to her man affectionately as "papi" (daddy) or "chulo" (cutie) unless she's upset with him, in which case he's a "pendejo" (dumbass) or "sangano" (idiot). Frequently speaks English (or Spanglish) rather than Spanish but conversant in both languages.

**MATING:** Fickle, sexy, and promiscuous while single, but extremely territorial in any exclusive relationship. Tends to have a non-traditional family structure and stay single longer than most other Latin American species. If she has a child out of wedlock — as often happens — she'll go after the biological father for child support until she gets it or they repo his ride. Known to wait one night to two weeks before closing the deal.

**MAGNETS:** Attracted mainly to Latin and black guys, especially bad boys and players. Occasionally dates other types with a compatibly urban lifestyle and worldview.

**HABITAT:** Dominican hair salon; party; concert; local (urban) club, restaurant, or shop; National Puerto Rican Day Parade in New York City.

**LOCATION:** Abundant to common in New York, especially New York City, with the largest Puerto Rican community outside Puerto Rico, and the Bronx; New Jersey, especially Camden, Perth Amboy, Newark, and Vineland; Pennsylvania, especially Lancaster, Reading, Allentown, and (North) Philadelphia; Massachusetts, especially Holyoke, Springfield, and Lawrence; Connecticut, especially Hartford, Bridgeport, and New Britain; and parts of (central and northern) Florida, especially Orlando; Cleveland-Lorain- Elyria, Ohio; and Chicago, Illinois.

**MIGRATION:** Somewhat migratory.

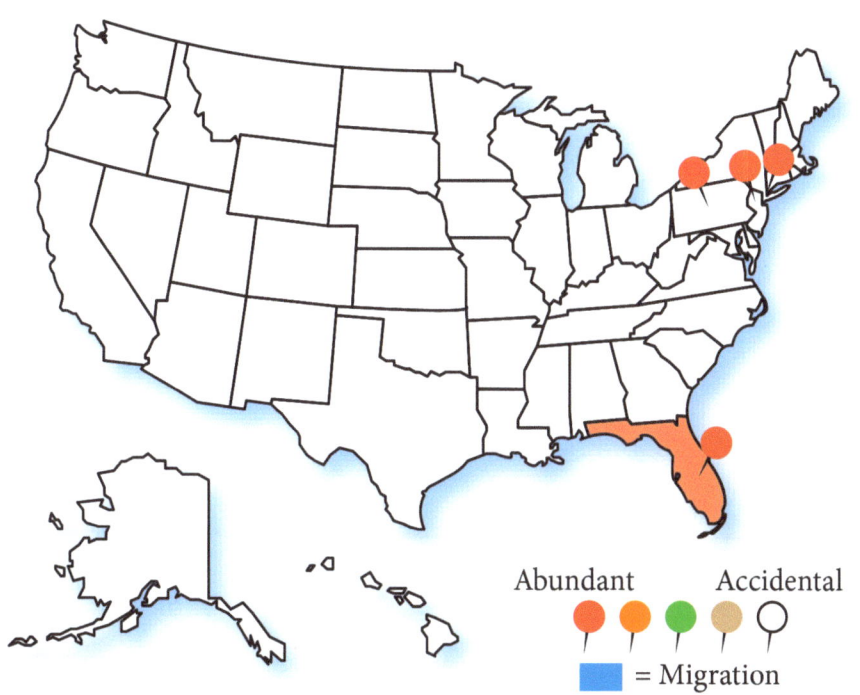

Abundant　　Accidental

☐ = Migration

CHICASPOTTING

JOE BOVINO

# TRIFECTA™
(Venezuelan American)

**APPEARANCE:** Also known as "Miss Venezuela" or "La Perfecta," this high-stakes chica is always beauty-pageant ready, no matter how old she is. Normally medium-height — and slightly taller than the Colombian American *Symmetrical Force* if you're having trouble telling the difference — with a lean, curvy body; olive or bronzed skin (with optional freckles, especially on her chest, back, or shoulders); long, dark (or bleached blond) hair; and expressive eyes. Natural breasts tend to be small to medium-sized, but large fake boobs are common. Doesn't hesitate to get a nose job or other cosmetic surgery either. Dresses with style and tries to look sexy at all times without over-accessorizing.

## ONLY SMOKING HOT WILL DO

Some of the most beautiful women in the world compete to win the Miss Venezuela beauty pageant every year, and the American version is trying to keep up. This competitive spirit often translates into stunningly good looks.

## NOTABLES

Michelle Lewin, Chiquinquirá Delgado, Cristina Abuhazi, Anabelle Blum, Patricia Velásquez, Génesis Rodríguez (1/2 *Transformer*), Majandra Delfino, and Jacqueline Marquez.

**SONG:** Seductive Spanish accent.

**BEHAVIOR:** Confident, (brutally) honest, proud, and poised — like the beauty pageant winner she is (in her mind) or wants to be. Engaging and demure but narcissistic, condescending, and callous at times, even if she's not that pretty. Often well-educated, industrious, and ambitious but family-oriented, well-rounded, and religious (mainly Catholic). Emotional with friends and family but somewhat quiet and introverted around strangers.

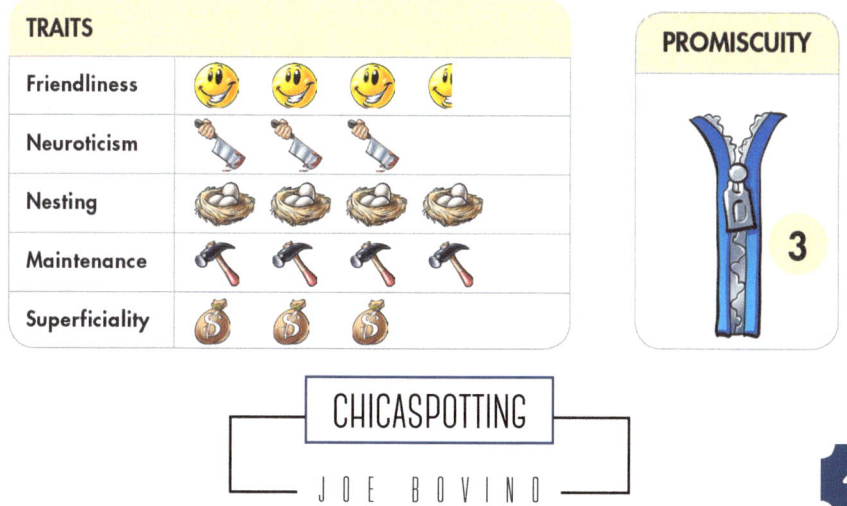

## NOT JUST ANOTHER REALLY PRETTY FACE

The Trifecta normally isn't content to rely on her good looks to get ahead. She's just as likely to be an engineer, professional, or entrepreneur as a model, actress, or beauty queen.

**MATING:** Routinely causes an erection lasting more than four hours, but neediness, jealousy, and controlling behavior — a real "Trifecta" of drama — occasionally spoil the mood. (The Venezuelan slang word for a very jealous or ill-tempered woman is "Cuaima.") If you're fortunate enough to get her into bed and make all the right moves, she'll return the favor and more. Just brace yourself for the talent competition. Known to wait one or two months before closing the deal.

**MAGNETS:** Attracted to gentlemen who treat her like the most beautiful woman in the world. Often dates Latin or white men who are respectful, protective, and capable of settling down. Expects you to treat waiters, housekeepers, and others with dignity and respect too, especially in her presence. Charming and charismatic risk-takers also have an edge, especially when the risks pay off in financial success.

## ADD SOME SALT

If you're white, the Trifecta is likely to assume that you're "una papa sin sal" (a potato without salt) — in other words, boring. Prove her wrong by taking risks and doing some things just for the fun of it. Stand out from the other potatoes.

**HABITAT:** Beauty salon; beauty pageant or competition; modeling or casting agency; gym; pool; Catholic church; mall; university; office building; beach; yacht or nice boat.

**LOCATION:** Common to somewhat common in South Florida, especially in the suburbs of Doral, Weston, Fontainebleau, The Hammocks, Key Biscayne, North Bay Village, Sunny Isles Beach, and Miami Beach. Casual in New York City and Los Angeles.

**MIGRATION:** Migratory.

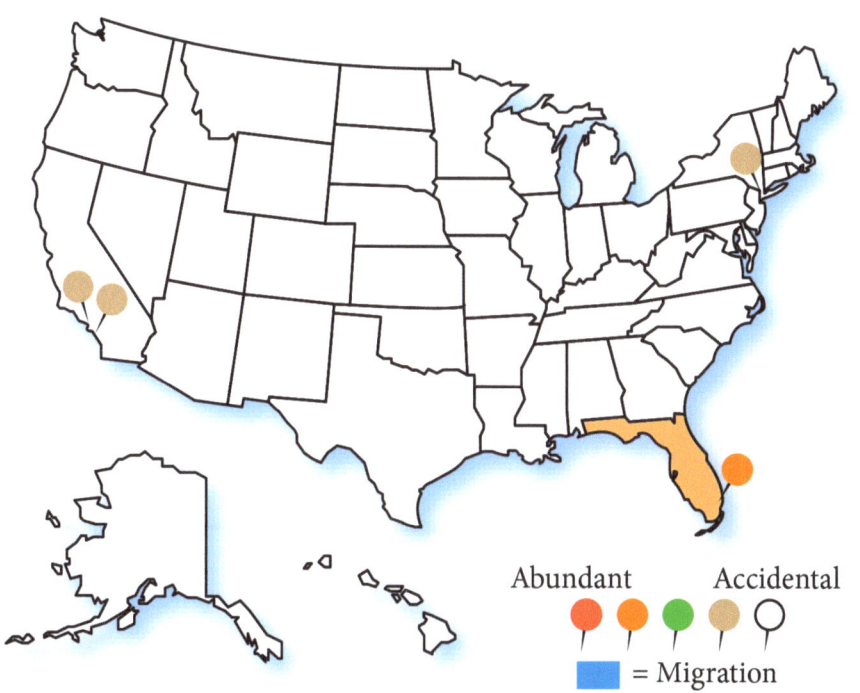

| Abundant | | | | Accidental |

■ = Migration

CHICASPOTTING

JOE BOVINO

# TRANSFORMER™
(Cuban American)

CHICASPOTTING — JOE BOVINO

**APPEARANCE:** This fiery Latina is recognizable by her "thick" hips and thighs, big shapely butt, small waist, and short upper body. She also tends to have brown or dyed blond hair, a round face, and brown, oval-shaped eyes. Skin tone ranges from fair to dark brown depending on her mix of Spanish and African ancestry. As comfortable in a business suit as a bikini. Dresses to look sexy and draw attention to her best assets, even if she's fat, because she thinks she's hot either way.

## WATCH THE KIDS AND CALS

If her breasts are large enough to match her hips and butt, the Transformer can be a Latin Jessica Rabbit, but too much Cuban food or too many kids and she'll transform into Rosie O'Donnell right before your eyes.

## NOTABLES

Eva Mendes, María Canals Barrera, Josie Loren, Génesis Rodríguez (1/2 *Trifecta*), Bella Thorne, Natalie Martinez, Christina Milian, Cameron Diaz (1/2 San Diegan *She Surfs, She Scores*), Ana Karla Suarez (not American, but wow), and Daisy Fuentes.

**BEHAVIOR:** Normally extroverted, friendly, and fun-loving, but headstrong and dominant. Tends to be reasonably well-educated but (overly) contentious and bumptious at times, especially if she's young and lower-class. Family-oriented and religious (mainly Catholic) but savvy, street-smart, and assiduous. Naturally musical.

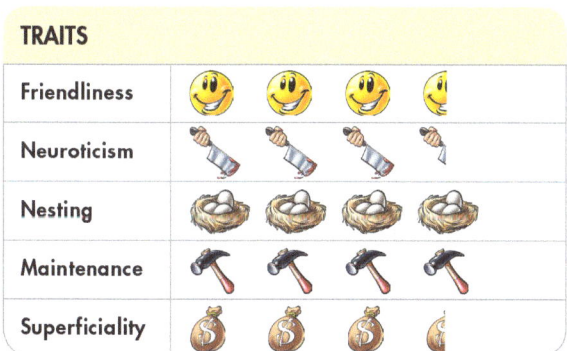
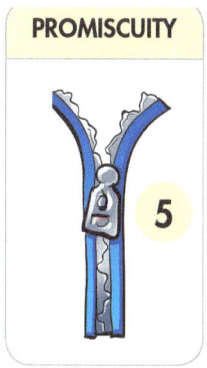

**SONG:** Outspoken, highly opinionated, and political. Exceptionally loud at times. Gestures frequently with her arms and hands while speaking any language. Speaks Spanish with a thick Cuban accent that even non-Cuban Latinos can't understand at times.

**MATING:** Even more aggressive than a Cuban guy when she's in an exclusive relationship. Intensely passionate, sensual, and caring but jealous, demanding, and possessive, sometimes exceptionally so. Playful in bed, where sex becomes an outlet for her pent-up feelings of love and lust. Known to wait one month (more or less) before closing the deal.

## THE ULTIMATE FIGHTER

This chica stays in charge and gets what she wants from a relationship, no matter what. If she has to fight to get it, so be it. Stand in her way at your own risk.

**MAGNETS:** Attracted mainly to successful Latin guys, especially muscle-bound Cuban-American ones. Occasionally dates white guys with similar traits and characteristics. Men who can dance well also have an edge.

## YOU SNOOZE, YOU LOSE

The Transformer expects you to take the initiative because that's what Cuban guys do, especially the older ones. If you wait for her to do more than flirt from a distance, she'll assume that you're disinterested, timid, ill-mannered, or insecure, none of which are desirable.

## DANCING WITH THE TRANSFORMERS

If you're serious about attracting and dating a Transformer, learn to salsa. It ain't easy because Latin guys show-off like peacocks on the dance floor. But non-Latin can men score big points by taking some lessons, getting out there, stepping on a few toes, and having fun. Perfection isn't necessary.

**HABITAT:** (Salsa) dance club or lesson; (private) party; Cuban café, cigar room, or restaurant; office building; college campus; political event; Catholic Church; beach.

**LOCATION:** Abundant in south FL, especially Westchester, Hialeah, Coral Terrace, West Miami, University Park, Olympia Heights, Tamiami, Hialeah Gardens, Medley, Sweetwater, Palm Springs North, Miami Lakes, Kendall Lakes, Fontainebleau, Miami, Coral Gables, Kendall, and Miami Beach. Common in West New York. Somewhat common in northern NJ.

**MIGRATION:** Somewhat migratory.

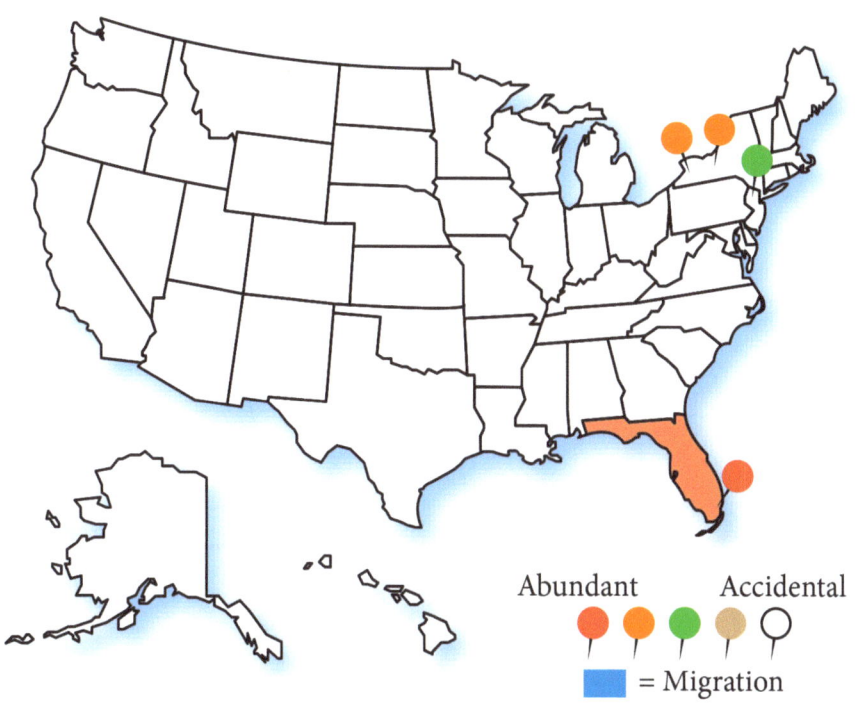

Abundant　　　Accidental

= Migration

CHICASPOTTING

JOE BOVINO

# PERUSIAN™
(Peruvian American)

**APPEARANCE:** Ethnically ambiguous fusion of Mestizo, Amerindian, and Spanish descent, but occasionally pure or mixed Chinese or Japanese, part Afro-Peruvian, or even Arab. Normally has more of a cylindrical than hourglass shape, with a relatively wide waist, a long butt, short legs, and naturally small to medium-sized breasts. Usually rather slender or average-sized but the cylinder gets considerably wider at times. Often appears top-heavy after a boob job because her booty isn't plump enough to balance things out. Other field marks include a relatively big head, roundish face, high cheekbones, slightly slanted eyes, large mouth, slightly "tosco" (rough) nose and lips, and light brown, bronzed, or olive-tinged skin.

## 1/3 (EXOTIC) ASS

If you see a chica who's practically 1/3 ass (vertically speaking) with a distinctively cylindrical shape, big head, short legs, (light) brown skin similar to other Latinas, and *slightly slanted eyes*, chances are she's a Perusian. If not, who cares? Go talk to her anyway.

## NOTABLES

Daniella Alonso (1/2 *Nuyorican*), Silvana Arias, Juana Burga Cervera, Alexis Amore, Isis Taylor, and Natalie Vertiz.

**BEHAVIOR:** Cheerful and easy-going most of the time but hot-tempered (if she catches you checking out other chicas) and prone to mood swings. Humble, traditional, and conservative in many ways. Often straightforward and religious (predominantly Catholic). Loves to eat great food (including ceviche), drink pisco, listen to huayño, and in some cases, surf. Generally well-educated, and hardworking (if necessary) but nevertheless prefers to marry a financially stable guy and stay at home with the kids.

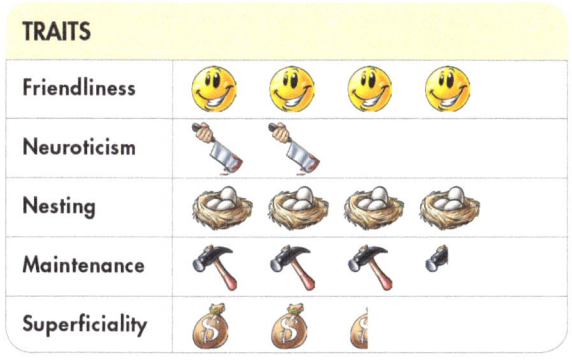
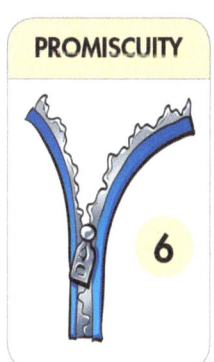

**SONG:** Loves to sing (the same old Latino summer hits) even if her voice sucks. Laughs frequently.

## THE HUMAN LIE DETECTOR

The Perusian places a high value on sincerity and will watch you like a hawk to see if you measure up. She may also (secretly) monitor your text messages, emails, voicemails, and/or social media profiles for evidence of dishonesty. So beware. If she catches you in a lie, you're toast.

**MATING:** Romantic, sensual, and aggressive in pursuit of eligible bachelors but possessive, jealous (at times), and cautious about pre-marital sex until she's officially your "novia" (girlfriend) or otherwise trusts you. Wild and up for anything in the sack once she does. Known to wait three to six weeks before closing the deal.

**MAGNETS:** Attracted mainly to white, Latin, and Middle-Eastern gentlemen who treat her like a princess and make her feel like one, especially if they're well-educated and financially stable. Strongly prefers (ostensibly) sincere men of high moral character. Rarely resorts to blatant gold digging but occasionally tries to outsmart the system in search of a visa.

**HABITAT:** Beach; restaurant; hotel; (dance) club or lounge; beauty salon; office building; pool; (private) party.

**LOCATION:** Common to somewhat common in New Jersey, especially East Newark (borough), Harrison, Paterson, Kearny, and Prospect Park. Somewhat common to casual in Florida, especially Hammocks, Virginia Gardens, Bay Harbor Islands, Doral, Key Biscayne, North Bay Village, Ojus, Kendal, and Kendal Lakes; and New York, especially Port Chester, Glen Cove, Rye, Elmsford, and White Plains.

**MIGRATION:** Migratory.

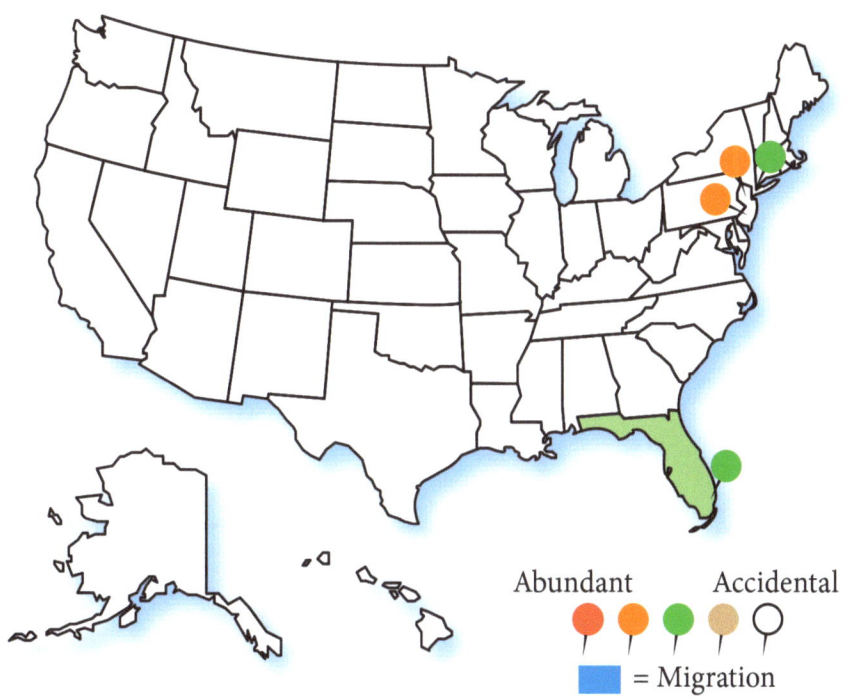

Abundant — Accidental
<br>
= Migration

## CHICASPOTTING

JOE BOVINO

# CINNAMON SWIRL™
**(Dominican American – Florida)**

**APPEARANCE:** Café latte or café mocha skin tone because approximately 73% of the Dominican population is mixed-race (black and something else), another 11% or so is black only, and many are tri-racial (with Taíno or Native American ancestry). Other field marks include: A small waist followed by a round booty on a short to medium-sized frame; an oval-shaped head (with puffy cheeks); long, naturally coarse black hair; full lips; big eyes; and a (slightly) wide or large nose. Breast size varies but implants are common. Nose jobs too. Usually well-groomed and fashionable. Carefully checks her outfit and accessories to ensure that everything matches before she leaves the house. Likes makeup, even if it's not necessary, and tight, sexy clothing to show off her body, even if she's fat.

## NOTABLES

Evelyn Jimenez, Aimee Carrero, Mirtha Michelle, Dania Ramirez, Iliana Ramirez, and Amelia Vega.

## SHE'S DOMINICAN, NOT BLACK

The Cinnamon Swirl often defines race by skin tone, including rubia (even if she's not blond), india, morena, and various in-between tones, but rarely refers to herself as black. If she doesn't do it, neither should you.

**BEHAVIOR:** Highly charismatic and gregarious, but stubborn and close-minded now and then. Drives as if traffic laws are optional and honks way too much at intersections. Often religious (Roman Catholic), moralistic, and superstitious but seldom boring. Usually from a large, close-knit, middle-class family that immigrated to Florida for greater freedom and economic opportunity. Tends to be reasonably well-educated, skilled, and entrepreneurial. Loves to sing (even on public transportation), dance, party, and watch baseball.

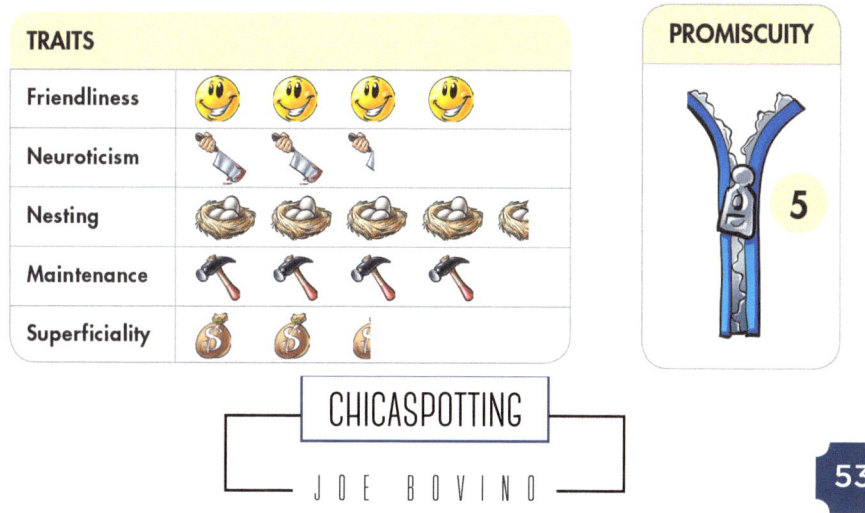

CHICASPOTTING

JOE BOVINO

## CHARISMA ENOUGH FOR TWO

Good luck finding a woman in the American field with more natural charisma than the Cinnamon Swirl. She knows how to have fun under almost any circumstances.

**SONG:** Chatty, gossipy, and highly expressive, especially among friends, but noisy and whiny at times. Giggles, smiles, and jokes around frequently. Peppers her Spanish with plenty of slang and abbreviations.

**MATING:** Ostensibly sweet, innocent, and loving but often secretly somewhat calculating, manipulative, and high-maintenance. Tends to be loving, loyal, and nurturing but equally demanding and dependent, especially after marriage. Sensual but rarely promiscuous because she prefers a serious relationship to casual sex. Wild in bed once there's a commitment but somewhat inhibited otherwise. Known to wait three dates to two months before closing the deal.

**MAGNETS:** Attracted mainly to tall, family-oriented white guys (with blue eyes), especially if they're romantic, respectful, and successful. Occasionally dates other types — especially non-Dominican Latinos — but seldom drawn to black men or others with darker skin tones. Often turned off by jealous or possessive behavior.

## WITH COMPLIMENTS

The Cinnamon Swirl is used to hearing piropos (compliments) from Dominican men and expects the same from you. So don't hold back. She loves the validation and wants to feel appreciated.

**HABITAT:** Dance club; party; (Dominican) beauty salon; Catholic Church; networking event; bar; restaurant.

**LOCATION:** Common to somewhat common in FL, especially Miami Gardens, Country Club, Carol City, Fontainebleau, Hialeah Gardens, Yeehaw Junction, Opa-Locka, South Miami Heights, Richmond West, West Little River, Virginia Gardens, El Portal, Miramar, North Bay Village, North Miami Beach, and Miami. Casual in NJ, NY, MA, and RI.

**MIGRATION:** Migratory.

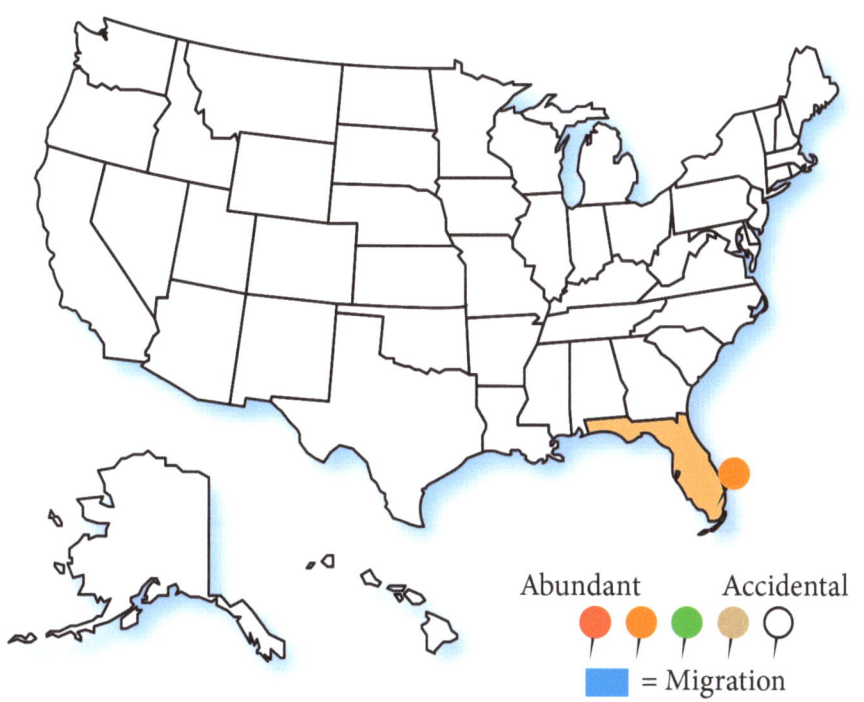

Abundant ● ● ● ● ○ Accidental

■ = Migration

CHICASPOTTING

JOE BOVINO

# BEAUTY CALL™
(Dominican American – Northeast)

**APPEARANCE:** Look for casual (but sexy) clothing, natural breasts (most of the time), good grooming, and other field marks similar to the *Cinnamon Swirl* in Florida, including a café mocha or café latte complexion, naturally coarse black hair, small waist, round booty, petite to medium-sized frame, a (slightly) big or wide nose, and full lips. Also tends to have an oval-shaped head and big, expressive eyes.

### NOTABLES

Adriana Diaz, Claudette Lali, Christina Mendez, Zoe Saldana (1/2 *Nuyorican*), Rosanna Tavarez, Omahyra Mota, Julissa Bermudez, and Miracles Espinal.

**BEHAVIOR:** Frequently visits or owns a Dominican beauty salon that caters primarily to Dominicans and other Latin American chicks. Tends to be energetic, spunky, and cheerful but lives, works, and socializes mainly with other Latinos, especially Dominicans. Normally comes from a family that resided in a poor rural town or urban ghetto in the Dominican Republic before immigrating to the United States. Typically hardworking, proud, family-oriented, and (somewhat) socially conservative. Often urban and inadequately educated, but there are an increasing number of exceptions. Loves to dance, party, and play.

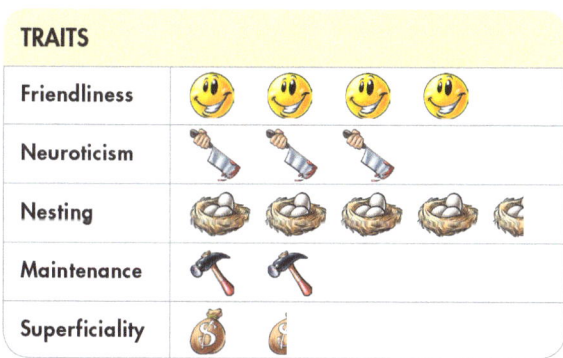
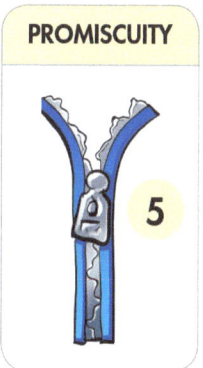

**SONG:** Verbose and opinionated but often somewhat inarticulate. Frequently curses and resorts to street slang. Gossipy, loud, and whiny at times.

## WHAT THE F*CK?

Zoe Saldana, the *Beauty Call/Nuyorican* actress who starred in the movie "Avatar" as a half-naked blue chick, "says 'fuck' slightly less often than Caroline Kennedy says 'you know,'" according to *Esquire* magazine. When asked about her ethnic Dominican background, she replied: "I hate that fucking question." She also noted: "That's why I try not to drink caffeine — it really fucks me up." Think twice before bringing this one home to meet your mother without a dress rehearsal.

**MATING:** Inclined to marry young and have kids right away because family matters most. Relatively low-maintenance for a lively, hot-blooded Latina who works hard and copes with plenty of stress on a daily basis. Known to wait three weeks to two months before closing the deal.

**MAGNETS:** Attracted predominantly to Dominican/Latin, black, and swarthy Southern European men but open to dating other types too, especially if they're cool, confident, or charismatic in some way. Far more interested in love, family, and (financial) security than luxury.

**HABITAT:** Dominican beauty salon; bodega; grocery store; garment shop; city restaurant or club; private party or any other gathering of friends and family.

**LOCATION:** Common to somewhat common in New York, especially Haverstraw, Sleepy Hollow, the Bronx, Manhattan, Washington Heights, Freeport (village), Copiague, Brentwood, and New York City; New Jersey, especially Perth Amboy, Passaic, Union City, Paterson, West New York, New Brunswick, Weehawken, North Bergen, Prospect Park, Guttenburg, Jersey City, and Hackensack; Massachusetts, especially Lawrence, Lynn, and Salem; and Providence, Rhode Island.

**MIGRATION:** Somewhat nonmigratory (except for trips to the Dominican Republic).

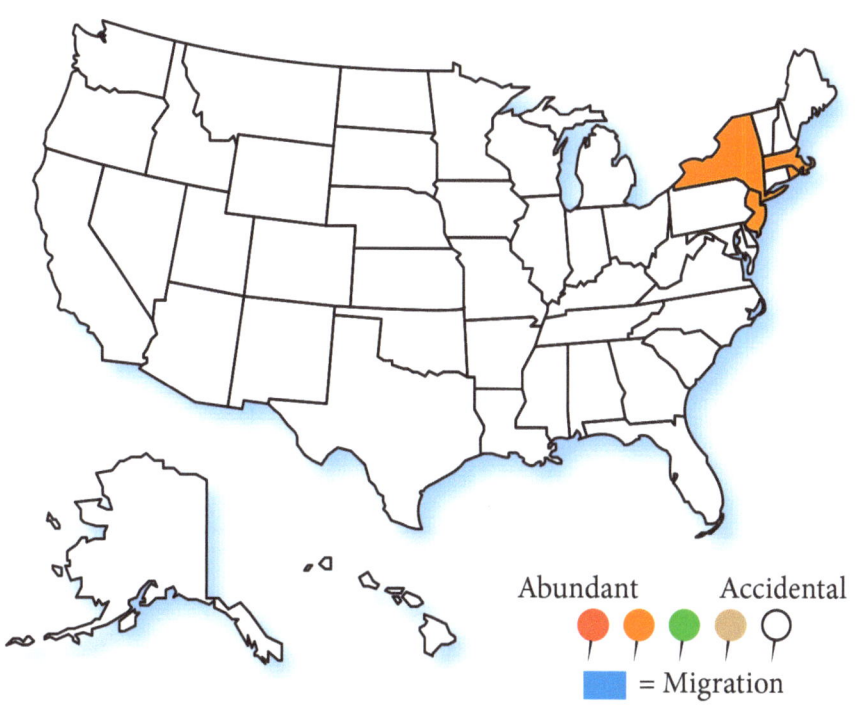

Abundant  Accidental

= Migration

CHICASPOTTING

JOE BOVINO

# PUPUSA™
(Salvadoran American)

**APPEARANCE:** The Pupusa [poo-poo-suh] is recognizable by her (somewhat) auburn-colored skin, big eyelashes, full lips, slightly wide or big nose on a round or oval-shaped face, brown hair, brown eyes, high cheekbones, and other features revealing some native Indian ancestry. Tends to be petite, average-sized or (slightly) overweight, with naturally medium-sized to large breasts. Normally takes it easy on the makeup — except for the eyes — and jewelry. Inclined to prefer simple, casual clothing over fancy or flashy attire.

## LESS IS MORE

The Pupusa tends to wear less ostentatious clothing and accessories than the Mexican American *Taco Belle,* if you're having trouble telling the difference.

**BEHAVIOR:** Hardworking — Salvadorans are often called "the Germans of Central America" — tough as nails, and religious (mainly Roman Catholic). Bright and optimistic but tends to sacrifice education and career to start a family at the earliest opportunity. More or less friendly but temperamental, cliquish, and bitchy at times. Loves to party and enjoy life but occasionally associates with Salvadoran thugs or gang members.

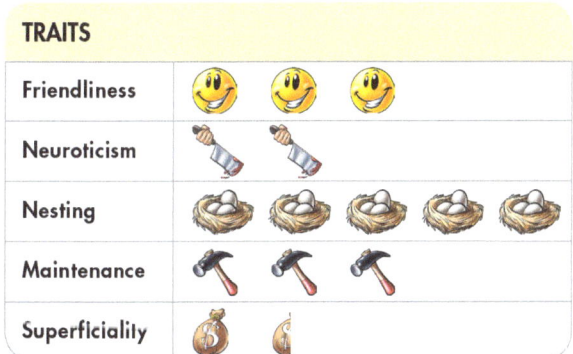
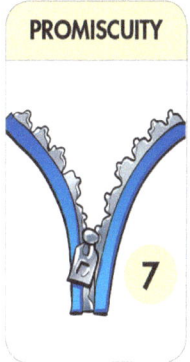

## WATCH IT, BUDDY

Mess with the Pupusa and she'll see to it that you never make that mistake again.

**SONG:** Speaks with a sultry slur. Frequently uses profanity, especially when angry or agitated, and likes to say "Bos!" (Hey you!). Often animated and loud.

**MATING:** Known for being a great lover who gets a man in over his head before he knows what hit him. Tends to marry young, have a few kids, and get fat. Typically sends quite a bit of your money back to family in El Salvador. Known to wait one date to one month before closing the deal.

## PUPUSA ADDICTION

Countless guys become addicted to Pupusa and end up hooked for life. Sleep with her in moderation or start saving for your kids' education right now.

**MAGNETS:** Attracted mainly to honest, hardworking men who know how to have fun. Open to dating outside her close-knit ethnic community but usually ends up marrying a Salvadoran or Mexican guy anyway. (Note: The Pupusa and *Taco Belle* often compete for eligible bachelors and like to claim that their men don't cross over, but it happens all the time and results in a lot of Salvadoran-Mexican marriages.)

**HABITAT:** Any Salvadoran event or party; nightclub; dance club; university; service industry job.

**LOCATION:** Common in the Washington metropolitan area of Washington D.C., Maryland, and Northern Virginia, especially Langley Park, Adelphi, Chillum, Brentwood, and Silver Spring, MD; Seven Corners, Bailey's Crossroads, and Herndon, VA; New York, especially New Cassel, Brentwood, North Bay Shore Hempstead, Huntington Station, Inwood, Uniondale, Freeport, and Roosevelt; and California, especially Mendota, Colma, the greater Los Angeles area, and the San Francisco Bay area. Somewhat common in northern New Jersey, Houston, Austin, Dallas, Chicago, and Chelsea, Massachusetts.

**MIGRATION:** Migratory.

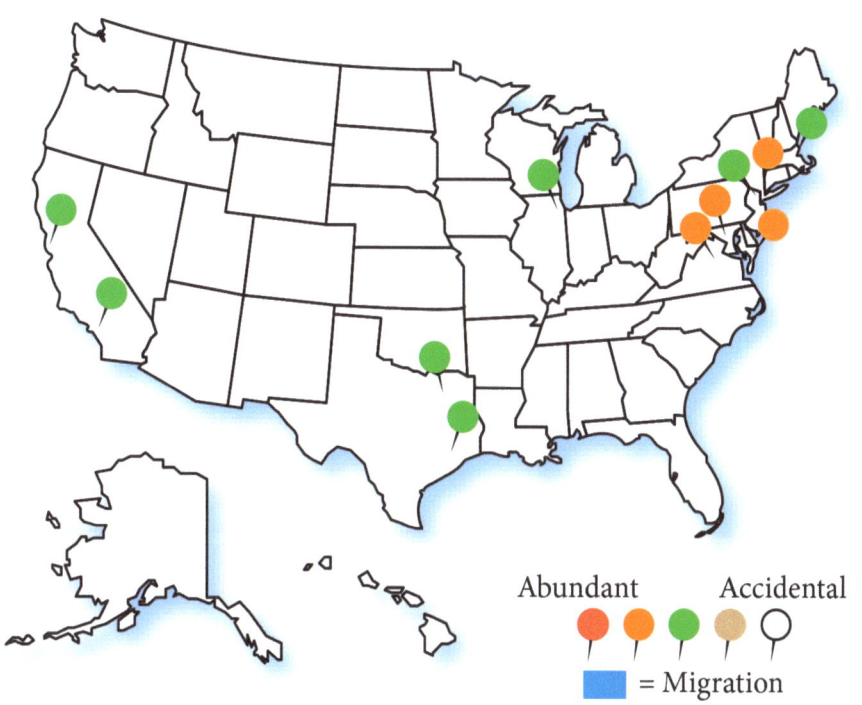

Abundant 　 Accidental

= Migration

CHICASPOTTING

JOE BOVINO

# HOTEMALAN™
## (Guatemalan American)

CHICASPOTTING

JOE BOVINO

64

**APPEARANCE:** Look for a compact, pint-sized body made to dance all night long, with small, perky breasts and a tight (at least slightly curvy) little butt. Typically balloons to average or plus-sized as soon as she has a child. Other field marks include distinctively Mayan facial features, such as high, wide cheekbones; big, slightly slanted, dark brown eyes; a flat, long, hawkish nose with a high, flat bridge; cocoa-colored skin tone; and straight black hair. Tends to dress sexy but conservatively and not wear a lot of makeup.

**NOTABLES**

Pam Rodriguez (1/2 *La Guitarra*), Martita Albarracin, Kalucha Chacon, Gabriela Salvado, Carmen Ramos, Denise Galindo (1/2 *Taco Belle*), and Claudia Rocio.

**BEHAVIOR:** Pleasant, serene, family-oriented, and traditional in many ways. Tends to be (reasonably) intelligent and understand the importance of a solid education. Often hardworking and somewhat religious (mainly Catholic).

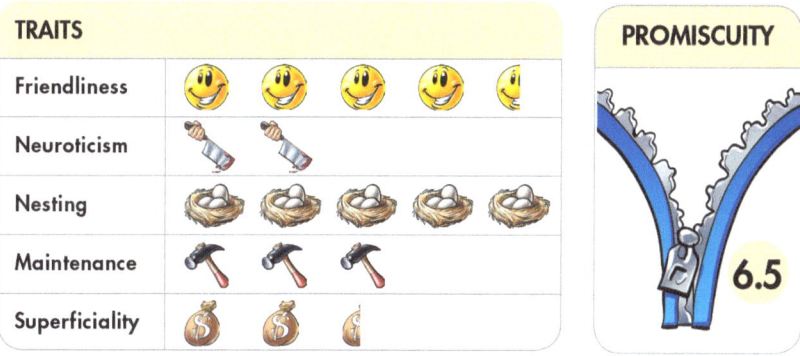

**SONG:** Relatively quiet and subdued around strangers but expressive and animated with close friends and family. Gabby and opinionated but rarely loud or pushy.

**MATING:** Mildly conservative but sensual, amorous, and red-hot behind closed doors. Normally doesn't sleep around, but not holding out for marriage either and will go for it occasionally if the chemistry is right. Womanly but really feisty, tough, and highly demanding at times. Known to wait one night to one month before closing the deal.

## ONLY YOU

The Hotemalan doesn't jump into bed with every guy she dates, but she may jump you (quickly) if you're genuinely interested in whatever she cares about and make her feel like the most important person in your world for a while.

**MAGNETS:** Drawn mainly to Latin or white guys who are financially stable, family-oriented, ostensibly honest, and relatively handsome (with a nice smile and beautiful eyes). Seldom dates Asian or black men.

**HABITAT:** (Latin) dance club and/or bar; soccer game; college or university; poolside; beach; church.

**LOCATION:** Abundant to common in Georgetown, DE; Ellijay, GA; Brewster, NY; and Langley Park, MD. Common to casual in many other places across the country, including but not limited to: Green Forest, AR; Chamblee, Buena Vista, Trion, Cedartown, and Canton, GA; Collinsville, AL; Indiantown, Lake Worth, Immokalee, Tice, Mangonia Park, and Homestead, FL; Mount Kisco, Jamesport, Spring Valley, and Port Chester, NY; Central Falls, RI; Schuyler and Lexington, NE; Morganton, NC; Fairview, NJ; Monterey, TN, and Los Angeles, CA. Rare in the Great Plains states and large sections of the Western United States.

**MIGRATION:** Somewhat migratory (if single); homebody (after marriage).

CHICASPOTTING
JOE BOVINO

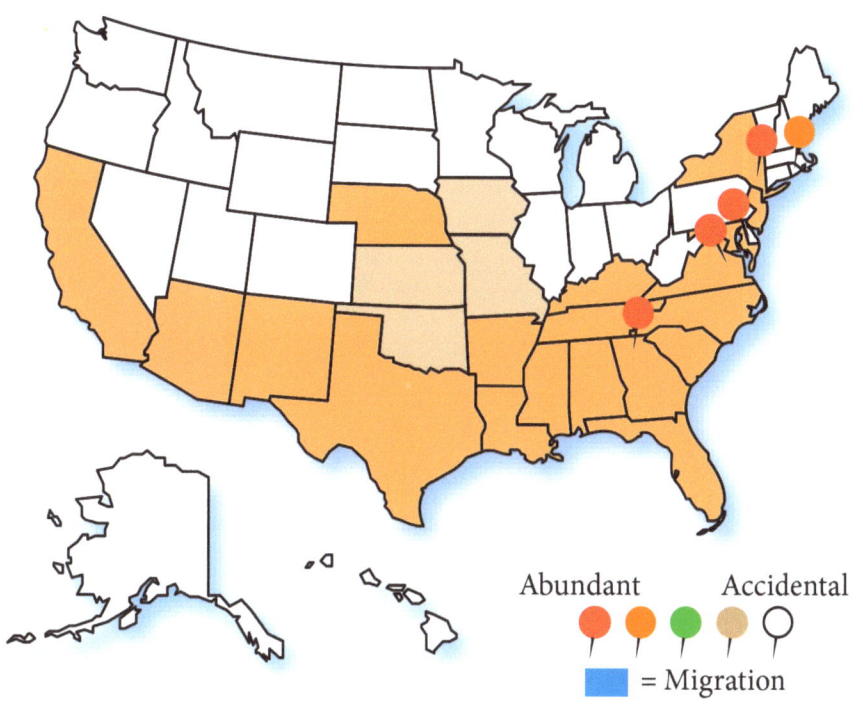

Abundant ● ● ● ● ○ Accidental

▮ = Migration

CHICASPOTTING

JOE BOVINO

# CONCLUSION

Thanks for reading the first field guide to Latinas of the United States!

I hope it leads to more enjoyable and fruitful chicaspotting.

And I hope it helps you to find, identify, appreciate, and *connect* with more of America's Latinas.

Drop a line to joe@chicaspotting.com to let me know how it's going in the field.

I look forward to hearing from you, especially if you've got an interesting or amusing story to share.

I also invite you to:

- Visit my website at www.joebovino.com;
- Like us on Facebook at www.facebook.com/fieldguidetochicks; and
- Follow me on Twitter at http://twitter.com/joebovino.

See you there!

Adios, amigos!

# ABOUT THE AUTHOR

**APPEARANCE:** Looks like the guy in the photo if the light hits him just right. Healthy and fit for a guy who spends way too much time staring at a laptop and smart phone.

**SONG:** Known to channel Dean Martin, Frank Sinatra or Michael Bublé at karaoke clubs with varying degrees of success. Tried to do the same with Tom Jones once and won't make that mistake again.

**BEHAVIOR:** Lawyer turned three-time #1 bestselling author and book publishing consultant. Appears as a cast member in the original P90X workout program and still exercises regularly. Loves his best friends like brothers but won't let them borrow his car or his girl. Enjoys international business, cross-cultural affairs (in various forms), history, politics, and satire. Dances better than your average gringo.

**MATING:** More player-coach than player these days. Master of international relations. (Well, not exactly, but he does have a Master of Arts degree in International Relations from the University of Southern California.) Loyal and ready to settle down but prepared to stay single if necessary, at least until he's too old to feed himself. Gold medalist in bed, no matter what she says.

**MAGNETS:** Prefers extraordinary women (who love his books and think he's awesome) to ordinary ones (who don't). No mustache is a plus. Irritable bowel syndrome is a deal-breaker.

**LOCATION:** Born and raised in Cherry Hill, New Jersey. Attended college in Charlottesville, Virginia and graduate school in Los Angeles. Spent most of the last twenty years in California and Florida (mostly Miami and Delray Beach) but travels often on chicaspotting expeditions.

**MIGRATION:** Frequent flyer.

Follow Joe Bovino on Twitter (@joebovino), Instagram (@bovinoj), and Pinterest (joebovino). Join him on Facebook (joebovinopage) and LinkedIn (joebovino). And visit his website at JoeBovino.com.

# CREDITS

## BOOK DESIGN

**Rick Soldin** (book-comp.com) provided book design and page layout services.

**Dr. Jay Polmar** of iPublicidades (https://www.elance.com/s/speedread) provided book design, cover design, page layout, print-on-demand, and eBook conversion services.

## ILLUSTRATIONS

**Linda Jackson** and **Darren Jackson** of DarlinDesign (darlindesign.co.uk) provided the following illustrations: Beauty Call, Bumbshell, Ecuadorable, Euro-Mina, Hotemalan, La Guitarra, Parts of a Chica, Perusian, Pupusa, and Taco Belle.

**Carsten Mell** (carstenmell.com) provided the following illustrations: Cinnamon Swirl, Nuyorican, Symmetrical Force, Transformer, and Trifecta.

**Christine Orvis** (cm-imagingstudio.com) retouched the Perusian, Symmetrical Force, and Transformer illustrations.

# NOTES

### INTRODUCTION

Malcolm Gladwell, *Outliers: The Story of Success* (New York: Little, Brown and Company 2008), p. 221.

Samuel P. Huntington, *The Clash of Civilizations and the Remaking of World Order* (Simon & Schuster Paperbacks, 1996), p. 20.

Peter J. Rentfrow, Samuel D. Gosling, and Jeff Potter, "A Theory of the Emergence, Persistence, and Expression of Geographic Variation in Psychological Characteristics," *Perspectives on Psychological Science* (Association for Psychological Science, 2008).

### SPECIES PROFILES

#### Taco Belle

Jada Yuan, "Belle Curves: Sara Ramirez," *New York Magazine* (September 18, 2006). http://nymag.com/arts/tv/reviews/21334/ (Retrieved May 10, 2010).

"Mexican Ancestry Maps," *Epodunk.com.* http://www.epodunk.com/ancestry/Mexican.html (Retrieved November 25, 2014).

"List of Mexican Americans," *Wikipedia, the Free Encyclopedia* http://en.wikipedia.org/wiki/List_of_Mexican_Americans (Retrieved November 25, 2014).

#### Bumbshell

H.J., "Brazilians: Portuguese for the perplexed," *The Economist* (May 24, 2013), http://www.economist.com/blogs/johnson/2013/05/brazilians (Retrieved January 4, 2014).

H.J., "Brazilians, ctd: More Perplexing Portuguese," *The Economist* (June 4, 2013), http://www.economist.com/blogs/johnson/2013/06/brazilians-ctd (Retrieved January 4, 2014).

"Brazilian Ancestry Maps," *Epodunk.com.* http://www.epodunk.com/ancestry/Brazilian.html (Retrieved November 25, 2014).

"List of Brazilian Americans," *Wikipedia, the Free Encyclopedia* http://en.wikipedia.org/wiki/List_of_Brazilian_Americans (Retrieved on November 25, 2014).

### Euro-Mina

James Bracken, *Che Boludo! A gringo's guide to understanding the Argentines*, Editorial Caleuche (2005).

"Argentine American," *Wikipedia, The Free Encyclopedia.* http://en.wikipedia.org/wiki/Argentine_American (Retrieved February 3, 2012).

"List of Argentine Americans," *Wikipedia, the Free Encyclopedia* http://en.wikipedia.org/wiki/List_of_Argentine_Americans (Retrieved November 25, 2014).

### Symmetrical Force

"Colombian Ancestry Maps," *Epodunk.com.* http://www.epodunk.com/ancestry/Colombian.html (Retrieved November 25, 2014).

"List of Colombian Americans," *Wikipedia, the Free Encyclopedia* http://en.wikipedia.org/wiki/List_of_Colombian_Americans (Retrieved November 25, 2014).

### La Guitarra

"Puerto Ricans in the United States," *Wikipedia, The Free Encyclopedia* (graphic by Angelo Falcón, Puerto Rican Population in the United States, 2000). http://en.wikipedia.org/wiki/Puerto_Ricans_in_the_United_States (Retrieved November 25, 2014).

"Puerto Rican Migration Patterns 1995-2000," *Wikipedia, The Free Encyclopedia* (graphic by Angelo Falcón). http://en.wikipedia.org/wiki/File:PR_Migration_1995-2000.jpg (Retrieved November 25, 2014).

"List of Stateside Puerto Ricans," *Wikipedia, the Free Encyclopedia* http://en.wikipedia.org/wiki/List_of_Stateside_Puerto_Ricans (Retrieved November 26, 2014).

### Nuyorican

*Movieline*, October 1996.

"Jennifer Lopez: 'Skinny Girls Miss Out'" (citing quote to *New York Post*), *US Weekly* (January 8, 2010). http://www.usmagazine.com/healthylifestyle/news/jennifer-lopez-skinny-girls-miss-out-201081 (Retrieved May 10, 2010).

See also "Jennifer Lopez," *AskMen;* http://www.askmen.com/celebs/women/singer/3_jennifer_lopez.html (Retrieved May 10, 2010).

"List of Stateside Puerto Ricans," *Wikipedia, the Free Encyclopedia* http://en.wikipedia.org/wiki/List_of_Stateside_Puerto_Ricans (Retrieved November 26, 2014).

"Nuyorican," *Wikipedia, The Free Encyclopedia.* http://en.wikipedia.org/wiki/Nuyorican (Retrieved May 10, 2010).

"Puerto Rican Migration Patterns 1995-2000," *Wikipedia, The Free Encyclopedia* (graphic by Angelo Falcón). http://en.wikipedia.org/wiki/File: PR_Migration_1995-2000.jpg (Retrieved August 17, 2010).

### Trifecta

"Venezuelan Ancestry Maps," *Epodunk.com*. http://www.epodunk.com/ancestry/Venezuelan.html (Retrieved April 17, 2010).

"List of Venezuelan Americans," *Wikipedia, the Free Encyclopedia* http://en.wikipedia.org/wiki/List_of_Venezuelan_Americans (Retrieved November 26, 2014).

### Transformer

"Cuban Ancestry Maps," *Epodunk.com*. http://www.epodunk.com/ancestry/Cuban.html (Retrieved November 26, 2014).

"List of Cuban Americans," *Wikipedia, the Free Encyclopedia* http://en.wikipedia.org/wiki/List_of_Cuban_Americans (Retrieved November 26, 2014).

### Cinnamon Swirl

"Central America and Caribbean: Dominican Republic," *The World Factbook*, Central Intelligence Agency. https://www.cia.gov/library/publications/the-world-factbook/geos/dr.html (Retrieved May 10, 2010).

### Beauty Call

David Katz, "Zoe Saldana: A Woman We Love," *Esquire* (May 2009), p. 92–95.

"Dominican Ancestry Maps," *Epodunk.com*. http://www.epodunk.com/ancestry/Dominican-Republic.html (Retrieved April 17, 2010).

### Perusian

"Peruvian Ancestry Maps," *Epodunk.com*. http://www.epodunk.com/ancestry/Dominican-Republic.html (Retrieved April 17, 2010).

### Pupusa

Jeremy Mumford, "Salvadoran Americans," *Everyculture.com* (Advameg, Inc., 2008). http://www.everyculture.com/multi/Pa-Sp/Salvadoran-Americans.html (Retrieved May 10, 2010).

"Salvadoran Ancestry Maps," *Epodunk.com*. http://www.epodunk.com/ancestry/Salvadoran.html (Retrieved April 17, 2010).

### Ecuadorable

"Ecuadorian Ancestry Maps," *Epodunk.com*. http://www.epodunk.com/ancestry/Ecuadorian.html (Retrieved May 10, 2010).

### Hotemalan

"Guatemalan Ancestry Maps," *Epodunk.com*. http://www.epodunk.com/ancestry/Guatemalan.html (Retrieved May 10, 2010).

www.ingramcontent.com/pod-product-compliance
Lightning Source LLC
Chambersburg PA
CBHW040101020526
44112CB00028B/57